THE AWAKENING MIND

THE FOUNDATION OF BUDDHIST THOUGHT SERIES

The Awakening Mind

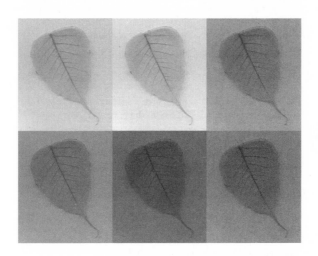

THE FOUNDATION of BUDDHIST THOUGHT

VOLUME IV

GESHE TASHI TSERING

FOREWORD BY LAMA ZOPA RINPOCHE

EDITED BY GORDON MCDOUGALL

WISDOM PUBLICATIONS • BOSTON

Wisdom Publications, Inc.
199 Elm Street
Somerville MA 02144 USA
www.wisdompubs.org

Library of Congress Cataloging-in-Publication Data

Tashi Tsering, Geshe, 1958–

The awakening mind / Geshe Tashi Tsering ; foreword by Lama Zopa Rinpoche ; edited by Gordon McDougall.

    p. cm. — (Foundation of Buddhist thought ; v. 4)

Includes bibliographical references and index.

ISBN 0-86171-510-1 (pbk. : alk. paper)

1. Bodhicitta (Buddhism) 2. Compassion—Religious aspects—Buddhism.
3. Bodhisattvas. 4. Spiritual life—Mahayana Buddhism. I. McDougall,
Gordon, 1948- II. Title.

BQ4398.5.T37 2008

294.3'420423—dc22   2008012117

Cover and interior design by Gopa&Ted2, Inc. Set in Goudy 10.5/16 pt.

Wisdom Publications' books are printed on acid-free paper and meet the
guidelines for permanence and durability set by the Committee on Produc-
tion Guidelines for Book Longevity of the Council on Library Resources.

♻ This book was produced with environmental mindfulness. We have
elected to print this title on 30% PCW recycled paper. As a result, we
have saved the following resources: 12 trees, 9 million BTUs of energy, 1,096
lbs. of greenhouse gases, 4,548 gallons of water, and 584 lbs. of solid waste.
For more information, please visit our website, www.wisdompubs.org. This
paper is also FSC certified. For more information, please visit www.fscus.org.

Printed in the United States of America.

Dedicated to my late mother, Dolma Buti.

CONTENTS

FOREWORD

THE BUDDHA'S MESSAGE is universal. We all search for happiness but somehow fail to find it because we are looking for it in the wrong direction. Only when we start cherishing others will true happiness grow within us. And so the Buddha's essential teaching is one of compassion and ethics, combined with the wisdom that understands the nature of reality. The teachings of the Buddha contain everything needed to eliminate suffering and make life truly meaningful, and as such the teachings are not only relevant to today's world, but vital.

This is the message my precious teacher, Lama Thubten Yeshe, gave to his Western students. His vision to present the Dharma in a way that was accessible and relevant to everyone continues and grows as his legacy. His organization, the Foundation for the Preservation of the Mahayana Tradition (FPMT), now has centers all over the world, and Lama's work is carried on by many of his students.

The Foundation of Buddhist Thought, developed by Geshe Tashi Tsering, is one of the core courses of the FPMT's integrated education program. The essence of Tibetan Buddhist philosophy can be found within its curriculum, consisting of six different subjects in Buddhist thought and practice. *The Foundation of Buddhist Thought* serves as a wonderful basis for further study in Buddhism, as well as a tool to transform our everyday lives into something meaningful.

Geshe Tashi has been the resident teacher at Jamyang Buddhist Centre, London, since 1994. He has been incredibly beneficial in skillfully guiding the students both in London and in many other centers where he teaches. Besides his profound knowledge—he is a Lharampa Geshe, the highest educational qualification within our tradition—his excellent English and deep understanding of Western students means that he can present the Dharma in a way that is both accessible and relevant. His wisdom, compassion, and humor are combined with a genuine gift as a teacher. You will see within the six books of *The Foundation of Buddhist Thought* series the same combination of profound understanding and heart advice that can guide both beginner and experienced Dharma practitioner alike on the spiritual path.

Whether you read this book out of curiosity or as part of your spiritual journey, I sincerely hope that you find it beneficial and that it shows you a way to open your heart and develop your wisdom.

Lama Zopa Rinpoche

Spiritual Director

The Foundation for the Preservation of the Mahayana Tradition

Preface

Looking back on my life, I feel both grateful and humble that I have had so many opportunities to learn about the wonderful awakening mind, called *bodhichitta* in Sanskrit, the mind wishing to attain enlightenment for the sake of all living beings. Not only have I studied the great texts again and again in the monastery, but I have also heard many precious masters such as His Holiness the Dalai Lama teach on the subject often.

Despite the little I have been able to assimilate within my mental continuum, I still feel my continued exposure to the teachings on the awakening mind has done me much good. I'm not sure how far down the road to altruism I have gone, but I am completely convinced from all that I have studied that were I to cultivate such a mind at some distant time in the future, it would have immeasurable benefits for me and for all those I came into contact with over the course of my lifetime. Moreover, there would be both immediate benefits, such as the freedom from the fears, worries, and uncertainties that are now part and parcel of daily life, as well as long-term benefits, such as attaining the fully awakened state of enlightenment.

It is very interesting how Western students, utterly unabashed, often ask His Holiness the Dalai Lama if he has such a mind, a question no Tibetan would ever dare ask. His answer, invariably given with great humor, is that he has been trying since he was a boy to get a glimpse of such a mind, and that the day he cultivates the mind of enlightenment will be the day he can finally take a good rest.

This answer tells us how crucial the awakening mind of enlightenment is, and it is not just the present Dalai Lama who understands its importance. There is a long tradition of teachings on bodhichitta and many, many generations of great masters have understood this, beginning with the Buddha himself.

All of the Mahayana traditions say that to achieve full enlightenment both the wisdom and the method sides of the practice are needed. *Wisdom* refers to the profound heart-level understanding of subjects such as selflessness, impermanence, and lack of inherent existence, and *method* refers to the development of the emotional, intuitive side of the mind—kindness, love, ethics, and so on. Paramount to the method side is the cultivation of bodhichitta.

Buddhism is both a religion and a philosophy, and within the Tibetan tradition great emphasis is placed on philosophical inquiry, so it is natural that over the millennia there have arisen many different views on how things truly exist. Each suits a particular mental disposition, and while none are in direct contradiction, together they create a spectrum of philosophical views. What I find very interesting, though, is that, despite the love of debate and questioning within our tradition, there is no disagreement about the mind of enlightenment. All traditions agree, and agree totally and without argument, on the concept, its importance, and the methods of developing it.

Without a mind utterly and continually bent on others' welfare, all our activities are sullied with self-interest. But the awakening mind is more than just compassion for others—it is the mind completely given to the aspiration of gaining full enlightenment as the only truly satisfactory means of benefiting all others in the utmost possible way. It is a huge mind. It is *the* most vast mind. With such a mind, every action of body, speech, and mind is pure and leads us inexorably toward enlightenment.

We should rejoice, because we are already taking the first tentative steps toward attaining bodhichitta, something so rare these days. If we have the courage, the route is mapped out for us. And it is a set route. Most masters agree that although there are different methods for developing this mind, there are definite steps that must be taken. These have been formalized over the centuries by Indian and Tibetan Buddhist masters into two main methods, with a third that is an amalgamation of both. They lead us to a mind that is imbued with a strong sense of love and compassion for all other living beings, a feeling of dearness and closeness to all. From that mind there arises the natural wish to help all beings in the most profound way possible.

Given it is such an important subject, there have of course been many wonderful books written by masters far more learned and accomplished than I, so I was at first quite reluctant to write on the awakening mind. But really there can never be too many books on the subject, and within the framework of *The Foundation of Buddhist Thought* series, this is a topic that must be tackled. Although I have no realizations of such a mind, perhaps somehow some little understanding has crept in over all the many years that I have studied it, and perhaps, because of my long association with Western people through teaching in the West, I can impart the wisdom of the earlier great masters in a language that is accessible and enjoyable. If that is the case, then presenting the teachings on this utterly incredible mind is a great pleasure to me. If, in this book, I can give you even a little of the inspiration the teachings of the great masters have given to me on this topic, then I feel I will have achieved my purpose.

Editor's Preface

OVER THE YEARS that I have been associated with *The Foundation of Buddhist Thought* course devised by Geshe Tashi in 1997, one aspect that often strikes me is how the different modules attract different students. Some students sail through the comparatively esoteric and difficult concept of the two truths covered in *Relative Truth, Ultimate Truth*, but find the idea of taking responsibility for the happiness of all sentient beings that bodhichitta entails terrifying. Some are comfortable with the idea of love, but balk when it comes to a love that understands reality, in all its gritty and not so pretty aspects. I'm sure, should you read all six books in the series, that you will have your favorites and ones you are challenged by. Hopefully you will also see how skillful Geshe Tashi has been in choosing these six topics to give a complete overview of Buddhism from a Tibetan perspective.

Mahayana Buddhism's prime foci are compassion—the wish that others be freed from suffering—and understanding reality so we can help make that happen. So therefore it is little wonder that the majority of the Foundation of Buddhist Thought students, attracted as they are to a Tibetan Buddhist course, find the awakening mind of enlightenment to be the most wonderful jewel of all. I found this subject a joy to study and edit.

Compassion and understanding, the two aspects of Buddhism that give it great strength and beauty, come together in the awakening mind. We each have different propensities, and are attracted to different ways of thinking, but within the term *bodhichitta*, the awakening mind of enlightenment, we are ambushed into embracing a mind so vast it breaks down our mental barriers. Those of us with a logical disposition can see how compassion is the only choice and thus learn to develop the intuitive, loving side of our natures; those of us whose minds naturally go toward love and compassion learn to see that the simple wish for people to be happy is pretty woolly unless reinforced with a deep understanding of why they are not, and so learn to develop the rational, understanding side of our natures. It's all here, and if we can even start to get a taste for this incredible mind, it can be the motivation to spur us into exploring all the other aspects of Buddhism, or any other great philosophy for that matter.

Many have been attracted to the course, and especially to the series of books, because of the "voice" of Geshe Tashi (a voice I hope I haven't dulled with my clumsy editing). It is a voice of warmth, humor, and understanding, but most of all compassion. Like his teachers, Geshe Tashi speaks only with the wish to help others, and his message of compassion and understanding shines through no matter what subject he is teaching.

I noticed this from the time I first met him in 1992, when he was staying at Nalanda Monastery in southern France, studying both the English language and the Western mind. When he studies an English language textbook, it is for compassion; when he reads *Scientific American*, it is for compassion. As he says, bodhichitta—compassion taken to its ultimate—is the essence of the Buddha's teachings, and so everything within Tibetan Buddhism leads back to bodhichitta. It has been Geshe Tashi's life.

Born in Purang, Tibet, in 1958, Geshe Tashi escaped to India with his parents one year later. He entered Sera Mey Monastic University at the age of thirteen, and spent the next sixteen years working for his Geshe degree, graduating as a Lharampa Geshe, the highest possible degree.

After a year at the Highest Tantric College (Gyuto), Geshe-la began his teaching career in Kopan Monastery in Kathmandu, the principal monastery of the Foundation for the Preservation of the Mahayana Tradition (FPMT). Geshe Tashi then moved to the Gandhi Foundation College in Nagpur, and it was at that time that the FPMT's Spiritual Director, Lama Thubten Zopa Rinpoche, asked him to teach in the West. After two years at Nalanda Monastery in France, in 1994, Geshe Tashi became the resident teacher at Jamyang Buddhist Centre in London.

Very early on in his teaching career at Jamyang he saw that the text-based, passive learning style usually associated with Tibetan Buddhism in Western Dharma centers often failed to engage the students in a meaningful way. By incorporating Western pedagogic methods, he devised a two-year, six-module course that he felt would give his students a solid overview of Buddhism. This book is derived from the fourth course book of *The Foundation of Buddhist Thought*.

As with the other books in the series, many people have been involved with its development and I would like to thank them all. I would also like to offer my warmest thanks to Lama Zopa Rinpoche, the head of the FPMT and the inspiration for the group of study programs to which *The Foundation of Buddhist Thought* belongs.

1 Awakening from the Sleep of Selfishness

The Essence of the Buddha's Teachings

BODHICHITTA IS THE ESSENCE of all Buddhist practice. The word *bodhichitta* itself explains so much: *bodhi* is Sanskrit for "awake" or "awakening," and *chitta* for "mind." As enlightenment is the state of being fully awakened, this precious mind of bodhichitta is the mind that is starting to become completely awakened in order to benefit all other beings. There are two aspects to this mind: the aspiration to benefit others and the wish to attain complete enlightenment in order to do that most skillfully.

In the Mahayana tradition, teachings of the Buddha are divided into three groups, or three "turnings of the wheel of the Dharma." The teachings on the awakening mind come from the second turning of the wheel of the Dharma, from the huge group of sutras called the *Prajnaparamita* or *Perfection of Wisdom* sutras. Although the explicit subject of these sutras is the nature of emptiness, or *shunyata* in Sanskrit, their strong implicit focus is on bodhichitta, or how to cultivate it initially, how to keep it, and how to strengthen it once it is cultivated.

To understand the implicit meaning of the Prajnaparamita sutras, Maitreya wrote a commentary entitled *The Ornament of Clear Realizations* (*Abhisamayalamkara*). Other commentaries on Maitreya's work soon followed, including Nagarjuna's *Precious Garland* (*Ratnavala*) and

Shantideva's A *Guide to the Bodhisattva's Way of Life* (*Bodhisattvacharya-vatara*). These commentaries further show us how crucial it is to develop the mind of enlightenment and enhance it by engaging in the bodhisattva's deeds.

Everything the Buddha taught is for the sake of developing this inestimable mind. As the great eighth-century Indian sage Shantideva says in A *Guide to the Bodhisattva's Way of Life*:

> It is the great sun that finally removes
> The misty ignorance of the world.
> It is the quintessential butter
> From the churning of the milk of Dharma.[1]

For me, this really sums up bodhichitta: just as fresh butter is the essence of milk when we churn it, so bodhichitta is the very essence of Dharma practice. Whatever practice we do on the Buddhist path, if we channel it toward achieving bodhichitta, then we are endeavoring to achieve the essence of all of the Buddha's teachings.

Shantideva's quote has particular resonance for me, as I well remember having to churn milk as a child. It was my daily task to milk the 150 goats my family owned and help my mother make butter. We lived in South India where it was incredibly hot, so this had to be done before daybreak. Being the oldest child, it was my responsibility to make sure we had fresh butter for all of our meals. And so I came to know the butter-making process very well.

Churning milk makes many different substances, such as cream, curds, and whey, but the essence is always the butter. Shantideva is asking us to look at our practice as the butter in "the milk of the Dharma," to understand that through understanding and practicing the Buddha's teachings we can gain many benefits; still, within them all, the essence is bodhichitta. It must be the core of everything we do.

There are many ways of studying and developing bodhichitta—reading, listening, meditating, and working with it in our environment. Ideally, we will diligently practice all methods with enthusiasm and vigor. But this is often much harder than we initially realize.

Many of us who have been following the Mahayana path for a long time will have already received teachings and initiations where bodhichitta has played a big part. From my own side, however, I can see how so often the mind of bodhichitta remains a superficial mind, a mind simply wishing to help others in the most general way. This is of course a wonderful mind, but it will not lead that far. It is like dreaming of traveling to India but in reality never doing anything to act upon our wish.

We need to find a way to go beyond that simple wish, and so we will be looking at two traditional and very effective step-by-step methods (and their synthesis) for developing the awakening mind. It is quite important—and very productive—to examine the procedure closely: the starting point of the process, what comes next, where that will lead us, and so on. By doing this, our meditation will not just be a wishing state of mind, but will become part of the process of actually achieving bodhichitta. The most precious mind of all, that which cherishes all beings, can become a genuine part of our life, a real gut feeling that motivates us in everything we do, and not just a vague wish.

What follows is like a manual: useless unless used as a practical guide to achieving your goal, the precious mind of bodhichitta. The words on these pages are simply lines of black ink unless they are somehow effective in stimulating the reader to take action, to begin contemplating bodhichitta in a systemic, vigorous way.

My hope is that by the end of this book you will feel that bodhichitta is the most important thing in your spiritual development, and that you will make a firm decision to actually develop it in a step-by-step way, taking your attitude beyond the mere *wishing* stage to the actualization of the mind intent on the well-being of all other beings.

The Benefits of Bodhichitta

A boat delivers one to the other bank.
A needle stitches up one's clothes.
A horse takes one where one wants to go.
Bodhichitta brings one to buddhahood.

The elixir called *the philosopher's stone*
turns the element iron into gold.
Bodhichitta turns this unclean body
into the body of a buddha.[2]

Buddhist masters claim that self-centeredness is behind all our suffering. Although we try to blame our suffering on factors that exist outside ourselves, such as our jobs, our families, and even global warming, Buddhism looks beyond this notion and ascribes it to the self-centered mind. If that is so, the solution must be the opposite, the mind that no longer focuses solely on the self.

Cultivating the awakening mind is the work of many lifetimes, and the goal might seem so far in the distance that we lose sight of it and strive for lesser ones instead. Therefore, from the very beginning, we need to establish the benefits of bodhichitta as clearly and strongly as possible in our minds. *This* is the motivation for everything we do, nothing less.

I recommend that in order to keep your motivation strong, you should habitually reacquaint yourself with the writings on the bodhichitta practice. In a sense, you should brainwash yourself into seeing that bodhichitta is the only worthwhile mind, and propagandize your-self into becoming a bodhichitta fanatic. We are all subjected to brain-washing and propaganda every day—literally millions of images bombard us, all to do with parting us from our money or bending our minds to another's way of thinking. But in this way, we are enforcing a kind of positive brainwashing, a deprogramming of the imbedded assumptions that are dominating our lives.

For this reason, guides such as Khunu Rinpoche's *Vast as the Heav-ens, Deep as the Sea* and Shantideva's *A Guide to the Bodhisattva's Way of Life* are particularly helpful in allowing us to refresh our practice and aspiration.

Shantideva's *A Guide to the Bodhisattva's Way of Life* is the most beloved book in Tibet. I have seen over thirty commentaries written about it, and His Holiness the Dalai Lama often quotes from it when he is teaching. Reflection on the individual verses stimulates and encourages the mind on its journey, like a key in a car's ignition.

The Tibetan Dzogchen master Khunu Rinpoche says:

> If you start something, start it with bodhichitta.
> If you think of something, let the thought be of bodhichitta.
> If you analyze something, analyze it in the light of bodhichitta.
> If you investigate something, investigate it in the light
> of bodhichitta.[3]

Lama Tsongkhapa also made this point in his *Great Treatise on the Stages of the Path to Enlightenment* (*Lamrim Chenmo*). He said that whenever he asked somebody what their main practice was they would mention some powerful deity, but he rarely met anyone who said, "My practice is bodhichitta." He thought that was very sad because it indicated the decline of the practice of Buddhadharma. There is certainly nothing wrong with having a tantric deity practice, but to concentrate on Tara, Chenrezig, or another tantric deity at the expense of developing bodhichitta is contradictory, as such deities are founded on bodhichitta. Without the motivation of bodhichitta, our entire practice becomes just another aspect of samsara, and there is no real benefit. With bodhichitta as your motivation, the benefits are infinite.

THE IMMEDIATE BENEFITS

At first the mere thought of an immeasurable mind that defies all superlatives is too daunting to conceive, and so it may be helpful to begin by thinking about the many benefits of developing bodhichitta, even on a very mundane level. By reducing our selfishness by even a little, we increase our happiness. So while we are striving for this vast and unimaginable mind that is our ultimate goal, we are at the same time effortlessly fulfilling our natural need to be happy.

The primary concern of bodhichitta is to develop a caring attitude toward others, and by doing so we will also reduce our attachment, aversion, and ignorance, the "three poisons" that are at the heart of all our suffering. At present our mind is ruled by partiality—liking one, disliking another, ignoring a third—but as we develop concern for others and our attachment, aversion, and apathy decrease, we will naturally become more content and happy. The selfish mind is a tight, unhappy mind, whereas the selfless mind is a light, joyful one. It is as if there is a continuum and we are somewhere in the middle, neither totally selfish nor totally selfless. Working toward eliminating our selfishness can only lead to greater degrees of happiness. While this may seem obvious, we have conditioned ourselves to seek happiness through external objects, such as a new car, a fun holiday, or an intense relationship.

The joy and lightness that we feel when we are doing something selfless is the exact opposite of the fear we feel when we are involved in selfish pursuits. The self-centered mind invariably exaggerates things. Objects of its desire become more attractive and objects of its aversion become more repulsive, and in both instances fear plays a big part—fear of losing the object of desire, or fear of the unwanted happening. It is a very simple equation if we consider it: selfishness equals fear and selflessness equals freedom from fear. The more we develop a mind that sincerely cares for others, the more that exaggeration will fall away, and the lighter and easier our life will become. There will definitely be less worry in our life.

There used to be a program on British television called 999, which showed reenactments of dangerous rescues people had performed. It was very popular because when we watch the bravery of people saving lives, we naturally feel an extreme sense of joy and pleasure. And this was just a reenactment on television of somebody else doing something good for others! If we ourselves managed to do something as altruistic, there is no doubt that we would feel real joy. And yet there is no way to compare that temporary accidental state of mind with genuine bodhichitta. In *A Guide to the Bodhisattva's Way of Life*, Shantideva says:

> If even the thought to relieve
> Living creatures of merely a headache
> Is a beneficial intention
> Endowed with infinite goodness,
>
> Then what need is there to mention
> The wish to dispel their inconceivable misery,
> Wishing every single one of them
> To realize boundless good qualities?[4]

We all know how grateful we feel when someone offers us even temporary, minor help, such as a pill for a headache, or advice on a computer virus. We should therefore feel so much more grateful to someone trying to develop altruism in order to lead us to the complete cessation of all our suffering.

And as we open ourselves up to the awakening mind, we become lighter and happier, less obsessed with our own personal problems, and have more space for others. Think about the people around us: our friends, co-workers, the men and women we see on the way to work. By cultivating bodhichitta, we are opening ourselves to bringing peace and benefit to all those we encounter. Our joy attracts them to us, and they feel a sense of calm and happiness in our presence, just as one smile can light up many other faces. This can spread to our community, our environment, and to the whole world.

So, no matter how immense the awakening mind of bodhichitta is, from this very moment it can start to change our lives, both positively and radically.

The Long-Term Benefits

If the immediate benefits of developing the awakening mind are wonderful, the long-term benefits are inconceivable. Shantideva says:

> All the buddhas who have contemplated for many eons
> Have seen it to be beneficial;
> For by it the limitless masses of beings
> Will quickly attain the supreme state of bliss.[5]

With bodhichitta our life becomes truly meaningful. Our present human body is the result of afflictive emotions and negative karma, and as such is a vessel for suffering, full of the potential for worries and difficulties. But if we can develop bodhichitta in this life, and become what is called a *bodhisattva*, this human body can become a buddha's body. Shantideva says:

> It is the supreme gold-making elixir,
> For it transforms the unclean body we have taken
> Into a priceless jewel of a Buddha-Form.
> Therefore firmly seize this Awakening Mind.[6]

If we manage to do something good for others spontaneously, even for a few seconds, we ultimately experience a feeling of great joy. This is not an abstract theory or a piece of random advice given to show us a state we can reach far in the future, but instead it is a simple statement of fact that I think we have all experienced at one time or another.

To put it simply, Lama Zopa Rinpoche often says that real happiness in life starts when we begin to cherish others. Bodhichitta will not only reduce our negative emotions, it will finally eliminate them completely because it is the main antidote to the self-centered mind. If all of our fears are caused by the self-centered mind, then cessation of that mind is key to our happiness. By cultivating this mind, every one of our actions is made worthwhile.

Without bodhichitta, even if we gain a direct realization of emptiness, it will not lead us to full enlightenment. We might achieve nirvana, we might become an arhat,[7] but we can go no further than this. That is why it is so important at the very beginning to set our motivations as high as we can, to determine that everything we do is for the purpose of attaining full enlightenment. And the sole reason we want to attain full enlightenment is to benefit all sentient beings.

There is no need to get as far as full enlightenment. The *moment* we generate bodhichitta in our mindstream, it is as if we are the daughter or son of the Buddha. Shantideva says:

> Today my life has (borne) fruit;
> (Having) well obtained this human existence,
> I've been born into the family of Buddha
> And now am one of Buddha's sons.[8]

That's really amazing, isn't it? To be born in the Buddha's family—how nice! How wonderful! Only then can we truly say our life is fruitful.

People claim that they are Mahayana practitioners because they study Tibetan Buddhism and do long sadhanas every day, but if they don't have a mind set on developing bodhichitta, they cannot be honest in their direction.

Lama Tsongkhapa says in his *Lamrim Chenmo* that whether or not our practice becomes a Buddhist practice on the bodhisattva path depends on our state of mind. If our mind is the awakening mind of bodhichitta, then even just reciting the mantra to bring temporary wealth will become a practice of the bodhisattva vehicle.

Imagine a life where all of the petty and not so petty concerns of self-interest no longer exist; where you are totally free from fear, worry, and indecision; where the wish to help others arises continually and spontaneously, and causes not heaviness and dread, but the most incredible joy, enabling you to have the energy and ability to make a profound difference.

Perhaps we can't really imagine what having such a mind would be like, but if we are lucky enough to have met the most accomplished Buddhist teachers, then we can easily see this in operation. His Holiness the Dalai Lama, Lama Zopa Rinpoche, Thich Nhat Hahn, Ajahn Sumedho—wonderful beings such as these—are living examples of what an awakening mind can be like. Utterly free of self-interest, they are invariably light, happy, humble, humorous, and above all totally compassionate and loving. They are the role models we should use when thinking about bodhichitta.

Why do people seem naturally drawn to people such as Lama Zopa Rinpoche? It isn't because he is from Nepal, or because he has a different face, or because he wears different robes. I think it is because he has that kind of mind. It is clear he totally cares for others, and so we love him and enjoy being around him. Because of his truly kind heart, his presence brings us so much joy. Our aspirations follow his guidance.

If this mind is so desirable, what can prevent us from seeking and eventually finding it? The answer is simply habit and conditioning. The habit of considering ourselves first has been with us for countless lifetimes and it has made us petty and weak, easily confused and easily manipulated. We see advertisements on the television for products such as fast cars, new clothes, and loud electronics, and we immediately are persuaded to think that we want, and need, these things. It seems so easy to manipulate our minds toward meaningless things and yet so difficult to point them toward spiritual things.

Even if a heavy smoker knows smoking will kill him, the habit is still hard to break. It is the same with the habit of self-centeredness. The habit is so strong because it is an addiction we have had for countless lifetimes. If we could truly understand our situation in samsara, we would see with shocking clarity how crucial it is to break that bad habit of ours, to stop being so easily manipulated by samsaric things and to start following the spiritual path. From my own side, I can see the huge gap between the logical understanding of the suffering nature of cyclic existence and the intuitive wish for comfort and pleasure. I cannot, at a heart level, see the fragility of the "happiness" I am now experiencing, and so my motivation to break free of the self-centered mind is still weak.

If a mountain climber halfway up a very steep rock face loses concentration, it is very dangerous. That is the situation we are all in at present: we are human beings and reasonably well off, especially from the material point of view of the West. At present, because of these transient material things supporting us, we seem quite safe and comfortable. But, even though it is certain that our support is going to disappear, we lack awareness of this. If we could really understand how unaware we are, that might be the shock we need to break the bad habit of relying on such things, and it could be the thing needed to encourage us to develop spiritually.

What is very clear is that we *can* train to have this mind called *bodhichitta*. It is possible. And if we have this kind of mind, there is no doubt it will be the source of true happiness for ourselves and for others. Ultimately it will lead us to full enlightenment, but more immediately the awakening mind can bring huge benefits to ourselves and others, as well as so much joy.

2 STEPS
ON THE PATH

FOR MANY OF US, a critical part of our Buddhist identity involves a spiritual pilgrimage to Bodhgaya. Such a journey requires months of preparation. We must consult with our Dharma teachers, chart out the pilgrimage, save our money and create a budget, arrange for transportation and lodging, and do all the necessary paperwork. All of this takes an incredible amount of energy and determination before even stepping foot on a plane.

In this sense, we know how to prepare for the task at hand. We may not know, however, that there are also clearly defined steps along the road to bodhichitta, aiding us in our personal, mental journey to the awakened mind.

Like going on a pilgrimage, we must also rearrange our lives through preparation and practice. There are three set stages for developing the awakening mind necessary for all individuals, and they have been formalized into three methods traditionally taught in Tibetan monasteries. The first involves the *seven points of cause and effect*, which allows us to contemplate compassion for others in order to generate the awakening mind. The second stage involves *equalizing and exchanging ourselves with others*, pushing us to contemplate samsara outside of our own beings and sensations. And finally, the third stage is a method that combines the first and second stages through a rigorous and disciplined approach. But in the same way that we must initially prepare to go on a pilgrimage, we have a great amount of work to do before taking on the responsibility of freeing all beings from suffering and leading them to ultimate peace. Developing the awakening mind takes time, skill, and determination, and there are preliminaries to prepare first: renunciation, stability, and equanimity.

Renunciation and Stability

As we discussed in the previous chapter, we can never think about cultivating the awakening mind until we have a clear, strong motivation to overcome all of the difficulties we will face. This involves rearranging our lives and renouncing those things that hinder our paths (the petty, ego-related concerns) and developing those that help us (the clear, concentrated mind that has the strength to transform itself).

Our first step in this direction involves developing a strong understanding of the true nature of cyclic existence—how we are governed by mental afflictions that condition everything we do and trap us in the ever-repeating series of causes and results called *samsara*. Life after life we go through this process, endlessly enduring suffering both major and minor, physical and mental. To understand this is not to adopt a fatalistic philosophy or dogma aimed at developing meekness and morality. We simply push our minds to understand the reality of our situations and then strive to overcome it. It is only when we clearly see the truth of our conditioned existence that we will have the desire to be free of it, able to actively do something about the situation, and wish to help all others who are in the same position.

As we contemplate cyclic existence and suffering, we find ourselves becoming frustrated with the petty, ego-driven desires and aversions that dominate and trap us in a cycle of neediness. Understanding the true nature of samsara, we begin to rise above it, generating a desire that is wholly aimed at benefiting and helping others. This is referred to as *renunciation*, although it has nothing to do with denying ourselves pleasure, the usual Western connotation, but instead involves lifting ourselves slowly out of the quagmire of conditioned existence, based wholly on an understanding of samsara.

The nineteenth-century Tibetan practitioner and scholar Gungthang Jampelyang left powerful advice for monks in various stages of their education. He said that life's activities are like ripples in water: as soon as one experience passes us, another is beginning, eventually multiplying infinitely around us. He then asked monks whether or not this is not the best time to immediately cut the cycle of unfinished activities and begin simplifying their already simple lives.

Many of us have dependents, families, and responsibilities that keep us from walking away from it all, but we all need to take the time to analyze our activities and see which are necessary and which are superfluous for survival. Not only do we not need these extravagances and add-ons, but we can easily see how they are binding us with attachment and aversion, entangling us in desire for short-term material wealth and gain. With inspection, we see that we can create a mind determined to free us and others from the power of delusion, anger, and attachment, bringing long-term benefits for ourselves and others.

Preparation is not a new concept for the Western student. We are constantly preparing for our lives, taking placement exams, applying to colleges, interviewing for careers, and finally striving to provide a comfortable life for our families. But at some point we begin to sense that there is something else we need to prepare for, something just beyond our grasp. There comes a time when we realize that a bigger house, a better promotion, or a faster car won't make us truly happy. There is always another step on the ladder, but we have no idea where it is leading us.

We realize how little of our hard work has been aimed toward the fulfillment of pure, true happiness when we see how unhappy and unfulfilled we really are. We see the flaws in our strategy, and decide to change ourselves at the mental level. By eliminating what is superfluous and time-wasting, we are giving ourselves the space to see the mind's real potential, leading us to a strong desire to develop ourselves. By concentrating on what has meaning, we renounce the worthless aspects of the life we have worked so hard to build.

This concentration and clarity provides the groundwork for our introspective meditation practice. This second preliminary, *stability*, is the ability of the mind to abide on one object without interference from mental distractions. Meditation, a term so many use but so few understand, means to habituate the mind to positive states, stabilizing the mind in calmness and clarity. This is in particular called the mind of calm abiding (Skt. *shamatha*, Tib. *shine*), and we will consider it in the next section, when we look at the equanimity of application.

Equanimity

Before moving forward into our practice of compassionate meditation, we need to develop a sense of equanimity in our minds. Our goal is to train ourselves in the seven points of cause and effect technique, recognizing that all sentient beings have been our mother, and feeling at the deepest level that there is no difference between ourselves and all other beings.

The term *equanimity* has different meanings, both culturally and contextually. Even Buddhist scholars cite three different types of equanimity:

+ equanimity of feeling
+ equanimity of application
+ immeasurable equanimity

THE EQUANIMITY OF FEELING

Equanimity of feeling is, strangely enough, not a factor in developing bodhichitta. Feeling is in essence one of the mental factors that must always be present as long as the mind functions, so if we are experiencing neither pleasure nor displeasure, there will arise a neutral feeling, or a feeling of indifference. As our aim is to cease the functions of a mind tied to the cyclic existence, this isolated and introverted mind disconnects us from others and as such does nothing to move us toward bodhichitta.

THE EQUANIMITY OF APPLICATION

While the equanimity of feeling aids us in understanding the body and mind we inhabit, the equanimity of application enables us to more fully develop spiritually, giving us the stability necessary to develop the third preliminary, immeasurable equanimity. It is a very advanced mind, the last of the nine stages of developing calm abiding, in which context it is called the *equal-setting mind*. By concentrating on the strongest distractions we face in meditation, we reduce the dull, sinking mind and the excited, scattered mind. The practicing Buddhist knows that this busy-ness is in fact a kind of laziness, a way of letting the mind escape the true business at hand.

IMMEASURABLE EQUANIMITY

By developing this equanimity of application, we come to see that we can use the mind as a foundation for developing the most critical form of equanimity. This third form can be cultivated within ourselves by one of two ways, based on either our wish for others' wellbeing, or on our relationship with others. In one sense, we contemplate the fact that all sentient beings around us are tangled in a web of self-induced affliction and hostility, and we develop a strong wish for all living beings to be free of samsara and its causes. In a second sense, we cultivate a mind that is truly impartial toward all beings, holding each relationship with the same regard and affection as the next. In effect, we treat all beings with equanimity and develop a mind indiscriminate of affection and aversion.

In the *Lamrim Chenmo*, Tsongkhapa advises us that:

> In this context, your meditation is on the distinction between friend and enemy. You do not have to eliminate the concept of friend or enemy, but the partiality arising from your attachment and aversion, based on the view that some people are your friends and some are your enemies.[9]

We can cultivate this immeasurable equanimity using a series of meditations, including examining the need of all living beings to gain happiness and avoid suffering, analyzing our own partiality, and seeing how harmful our actions can potentially be for ourselves and others. We become aware of the fact that in order to secure our own happiness, we can often block others from their own goals and joys. We realize that in grasping for objects and individuals, we make erroneous distinctions between friends and enemies, the partiality obscuring our clarity and causing harm. But by meditating on this partial mind, we bring ourselves closer to immeasurable equanimity.

The Buddhist scriptures state that we should feel equally close to all sentient beings, so often it may feel as if we are meant to distance ourselves from our good friends in order to cultivate this kind of equanimity. While we need to reevaluate our strongest relationships, we should see that it is most worthwhile for us to find ways of overcoming the attachment that is usually the reason for this closeness.

Attachment and closeness are two separate things, but often attachment brings about closeness. We know that we can never find equanimity if we are ruled by attachment, so we should therefore ask ourselves how much our relationships are ruled by love, and how much by self-interest.

Self-interest plays a very large part in many of our personal relationships. A person helps me in some way—perhaps by stroking my ego, by being my friend and making me feel worthwhile, or by helping me get something I want—and so I feel "close" to him or her. While the help this person may bring is real, the process is wrong: this person is special because she has helped me, that person is not special because she has not helped me. The mind exaggerates the quality of a person based on a very superficial criterion of help or harm. When we are honest with ourselves, we can see how illogically partial we are about other people, simply based upon how they treat us. This is true even of our spiritual teachers: we need to separate the closeness we feel for them from any attachment we might have developed. *Any* attachment, even to someone like His Holiness the Dalai Lama, is destructive.

In the same way, and using the same logic, we need to reduce the aversion we feel for the other class of beings, those who have harmed us in some way. Just as attachment to friends is unrealistic and narrowing, so too is aversion toward other beings. If we truly want to develop the mind of enlightenment, we need to include compassion for those who antagonize us in some way or another. It doesn't help to seek enlightenment for the sake of all beings *except* your ex-girlfriend or your landlord.

When my teacher gave teachings on this topic, he used the example of a nomad looking after a great flock of sheep. The sheep are all nameless and look exactly alike, but the nomad is concerned for all of them equally. There is no particular sheep he feels closer to, no lamb he particularly wishes to punish. It is our goal and mission to develop that mind for all sentient beings, going beyond the actual or imagined harm we perceive others to have done to us and instead seek the long-term happiness for ourselves and all others. With little reflection, we know that by obsessing on the short-term, superficial problems, we are destroying any chance we have to develop spiritually.

The Changeable Nature of Relationships

When we are finally able to see how we are continually pigeonholing people as "friend," "enemy," and "stranger," we can begin to understand the ultimate error in our categorizing mind. The implications of this error cause major damage in not only our present life, but in the life cycle that precedes and follows us from life to life.

Nagarjuna, in his *Letter to a Friend*, states:

> One's father becomes one's son and one's mother, one's wife.
> And the person who was an enemy becomes a beloved friend.
> Thus there is no certainty in cyclic existence.[10]

The meditation on equanimity is a method of breaking down this process of categorization.

Even the tiniest reasons will cause us to change our feelings entirely for a person. If a stranger gives me a big smile while riding on the bus to work, I like him just for that reason. But if he is in a bad mood the next day and ignores me, I feel shunned and hurt, as if I always knew he was a nasty person! We know that people who were once considered avowed enemies are close friends now. This is most definitely a factor of the constantly fluid, changing nature of our mind.

Through further meditation and contemplation, we also come to realize that even our attractions and aversions are not as simple and concrete as we initially suspected. Even those people to whom we have a strong aversion are people we also have a strong closeness with, even though this closeness exists only in a negative form at this stage. But with merely a small change, we may come to realize that this aversion can transform into a friendship given the right conditions. How often do we complain about our boss, that he is unfairly treating us? But perhaps were we to spend some social time with our boss, we would come to realize that his home life is a mess, and a kind word from us might turn his attitude around entirely, and change our initial aversion into sincere affection.

If we believe in future lives, then contemplating how relationships change from life to life is very helpful in developing equanimity. Not only does father become daughter and sister become uncle, but lover becomes enemy. Furthermore, in the context of future lives, the harm inflicted upon us now becomes quite superficial and short-term. At most it will last until we die, whereas whatever hostility we have created within our own minds because of that harm will cause us suffering into the next life and beyond.

When we are so obsessed with our own pain, we fail to consider others' positions and feelings. While we can easily forgive ourselves for becoming angry by saying "I was not myself," we often find it relatively impossible to reach the same conclusion when it comes to others' actions. Like us, they are not driven by wisdom or compassion, but by their confused and deluded minds. It is their delusion that is harming us. Seeing that this is so, we can finally begin to reduce our anger and aversion toward others.

The focus of this stage of our spiritual development is on bringing our thoughts and emotions into a more neutral state of mind. From this feeling of neutrality, we will be able to later develop a mind of closeness to all beings, friends, enemies, and complete strangers. We come to realize that they, like ourselves, want happiness and do not wish for sorrow. By equalizing our relationships with all sentient beings, we lower attachment to friends, reduce aversion to enemies, and become sympathetic to those outside our awareness. But our full aim is to move toward developing neutrality, and this is the next step in our stages of meditative development.

Lessening Our Aversion

Even when we can understand that attachment to friends and aversion for enemies are destructive minds, it is not easy to overcome them. In Buddhist psychology, the term *collective generality* describes the way this conceptual mind can overcome a whole group and form a general opinion.

We can use a spider as a wonderful example. Even without a picture, we can all form a mental image of a spider and feel a sense of aversion rising within us. When we consider this spider image in our head, feelings of dislike come to us naturally.

For Tibetans, we struggle with an aversion toward the Chinese. We logically know that individual Chinese people are the same as us, and it is only a relatively small group of leaders with a certain ideology who give the orders. Everyone else is as powerless against them in the same way we Tibetans are. But to so many Tibetans, it is all Chinese; there is that feeling of dislike triggered by the collective generality. We are all prey to stereotypes and prejudices, even if they do not manifest as racial hatred.

It is absolutely critical that we confront and overcome this subjection to the collective generality. We need to see the distorted feeling of aversion or attraction that arises when we apply to one individual the exaggerated general characteristics of a group, or when we rely on our own personal discrimination to cloud our overall understanding.

Often, we go as far as to let one incident inflict itself upon the "big picture," coloring our entire lives with anger and resentment, allowing us to bring negativity and blame upon further situations and experiences. We say things like "He has ruined my life by doing that particular thing," but we have trouble understanding that we are ruining our lives further by harboring hatred in our hearts. The harm continues long after the action has ceased, in much the same way the very idea of spiders continues to cause fear in our hearts.

Buddhist texts suggest two ways of dealing with this: by looking inward and seeing how it is our continuing aversion that is harming us now rather than the initial act, and by looking at the perpetrator and examining the motives behind his actions, and thus seeing beyond the harm done to ourselves.

Shantideva also gives us wonderful verses explaining the disadvantages of aversion and the advantages of equanimity in the sixth chapter of A Guide to the Bodhisattva's Way of Life. He says:

> There is no evil like hatred,
> And no fortitude like patience.
> Thus I should strive in various ways
> To meditate on patience.
>
> My mind will not experience peace
> If it fosters painful thoughts of hatred.
> I shall find no joy or happiness,
> Unable to sleep, I shall feel unsettled.[11]

This passage shows that we need to do more than simply *recognize* the fact that the mind of aversion is wrong, we need to realize that it actually *harms* us. This is not to say that we should act passively if we are being harmed by another individual, but we should restrain ourselves and act without anger or malice. When we counter anger with anger, a chain reaction is set in place; by countering anger with understanding, there is the potential for peace.

The Meditation on Equanimity

To begin the actual meditation on equanimity, start with a few minutes of breathing meditation, concentrating on the sensation of the air going in and out of your nostrils. This calms and focuses the mind.

Then, when you feel you are ready, visualize a good friend sitting in front of you. Bring up the feelings of warmth and joy that you usually experience when this person is near, and think about some of the things that the two of you do together, without letting yourself be distracted by any particular memories. Concentrate on the overall sense of that friendship.

Now, begin exploring your own mind in this relationship. What makes you feel so strongly attached to this person, this friendship? How is your love pure and unconditional? Or do you see some way you are benefiting in this relationship? Does this person make you feel intelligent, good, or beautiful?

Consider how anything less than unconditional love is dangerous in that it changes with conditions. If in this meditation on your friendship, you realize that some aspect of it relies on what that person provides for you, you must realize that it is a finite commodity, and it will eventually run out or expire. Love and attachment are two completely different things, and it is necessary to see each in our relationships with others. Our relationships are generally mixtures of love and attachment, and our goal is to decrease the attachment in order to achieve equanimity and understanding.

After you feel comfortable in this practice, move to visualize in front of you a person who is harming you in some way. While we are much too civilized to label these people "enemies," this should be a person who upsets you to a greater extent than most. It could be the neighbor who beats his wife, the mechanic who is robbing you blind, or an ex-spouse who is still demanding things from you. If no one comes to mind, it is also beneficial to consider world figures—

terrorists, politicians, representatives of something you feel is ultimately wrong in the world—and use them as your reference.

Again, as with the friendship visualization, don't dwell on the circumstances of this individual, replaying the soap opera in your mind. Instead, explore how your mind reacts to this. You feel aversion for this person, but why? How much of this pain and suffering is caused by his actions at one point in time, and not because the person is inherently evil? You should see that the aversion you are experiencing now is far more damaging than the harm this person originally did to you. By contemplating that, we separate ourselves from our anger and find that we can, in fact, manage it.

When you have fully explored this relationship, repeat the same practice with a stranger. You have no feelings toward this person: why? He or she most likely plays no part in your life, and therefore will not be an object of attachment or aversion in your mind. But it is not because this person is inherently uninteresting. It is a simple fact that we are so absorbed in our own story, and the "friends" and "enemies" that crowd that story, that there is no time for the myriad other beings that co-inhabit this planet with us. We hear of a tragedy in South America and might think how terrible it is, but, realistically, it probably does not touch us at all deeply. By contemplating why we feel apathy for the vast majority of beings, we can start to see how limiting and destructive our partiality is.

Once you have fully visualized these three separate individuals, it is necessary to take an interesting step further. At this point, you understand that what you intuitively feel as external intrinsic condition—good, bad, neutral—is only a projection of your mind, based on how that person has affected you. Now, however, visualize all three people sitting in front of you. Look at their differences. Perhaps your good friend has a sweet smile, the overbearing boss has a sneer, and the stranger makes no real impression on you. How many of your judgments are based on surface factors? By examining all three of them together, we can come to realize their similarities.

By visualizing all three, we can come to see that there are many small joys and disappointments throughout each individual's life. Probe deeper, perhaps creating whole histories, and begin to see the comparable experiences each one has gone through. Ultimately, they are sentient beings, their mindsets are created by delusions, and their deepest needs involve attaining happiness and avoiding suffering. The same suffering and happiness that plague us also act as the root causes of their actions, and that is why your friend tells outrageous jokes, your boss bullies you, and the stranger on the train buries her head in a book and avoids eye contact.

Our sense of equanimity grows when we come to realize how similar we are once we really contemplate ourselves with others. Common feelings at this point in the meditation involve lessened aversion for those we dislike and lessened attraction for those we enjoy. We might actually come to feel, as His Holiness the Dalai Lama often states, that "there are no more strangers, just people who haven't become part of our lives yet." But by repeating this meditation, either in formal situations or whenever you notice attachment, aversion, or apathy, the feelings of categorizations will eventually subside in ourselves and the intuitive feelings we have for people will lose their power in our judgment.

Once this feeling of equality becomes apparent, both in your meditative practice and in your everyday feelings, you will realize that this equalization will occur without discrimination or distinction. This is the first step—seeing them *all* as your dear friends can come later. At this early stage, the cost might be a slight distance from people in general, but the reward is an equanimity that can grow into boundless compassion.

While we are contemplating and comparing others, it is wholly important to remember that we must never stop observing our own behavior at all times. Watch your own behavior as you walk down the street and I'm sure you will find that you connect with certain individuals and recoil from others. This is a continuous process—we find ourselves smiling at adorable children in their strollers, but we try to stay far away from homeless men asking us for spare change. By working through this meditation, we are taking the various points of equanimity very seriously and diligently working to see the benefits of developing this mind of immeasurable equanimity. It's necessary to take this process step by step, being creative in our visualizations and developing a method that makes sense to our own personal minds. This is not, however, a process that we take up at the beginning of our practice and abandon later in life—it is a sequence of practices that will be helpful for the rest of our lives. This is the true core of Buddhism, and from this equanimity all other great minds can develop.

3 The Intuitive Route to Selflessness

The Main Mind of Bodhichitta

As a river to the sea,
as the sea to clouds,
as clouds to the land,
so does bodhichitta beautify this world.[12]

It is a part of human nature for us to have a profound concern for others. Yet so many of us are wrapped up in our own problems and desires, or those of our families, that we have little energy to be of any significant help. That you are reading these words is hopefully an indication that you have managed to go beyond that stage and are actually seeking ways to benefit others. Maitreya said in one of his texts that the wish to benefit others and to develop patience is a sign that a person's buddha nature is being activated. Our buddha nature, or buddha potential, is the love and understanding that lie at the core of our being, unsullied by any deluded minds at all. So this is an inspiring statement.

Many people think Buddhism is a wonderful philosophy but lack the time or inclination to look into it in any depth. The concepts that are the heart of Buddhist philosophy might seem very alien to a modern world, yet there is obviously some resonance for you that has kept you reading, studying, or meditating. Probably by now you are starting to realize that developing the awakening mind takes a very long time, so by persevering in your practice, you are developing patience, thus truly fulfilling one of Maitreya's requisites for activating the buddha potential within us all. You are so fortunate to have this kind of propensity to improve your mind. It is very rare and the cause of great joy.

THE TWO MENTAL FACTORS THAT MAKE UP BODHICHITTA

The mind is a combination of a main mind[13] along with a group of mental factors that come together, and it is the same with the mind of enlightenment. Bodhichitta is discussed as if it were a single mind, yet within that mind are various mental factors. Maitreya's seminal text *Ornament of Clear Realizations* (*Abhisamayalamkara*) is used frequently in monasteries for study of developing bodhichitta. In it he says:

> The cultivation of the mind of enlightenment
> Is the wish for complete enlightenment for the welfare of all
>   other beings.[14]

Here we come to understand the two mental factors needed to develop bodhichitta:

+ the sincere aspiration to attain enlightenment and
+ the altruistic intention to do so for the sake of others

When these two aspirations finally come together spontaneously through different techniques of meditation, the resulting mind is bodhichitta.

Initially, however, these two mental factors are weak, partial, and occasional. To develop them into strong, impartial, and continuous forces, and then further into the mind of bodhichitta, we need to rely on a specific methodology. Using the methods that make up the core of this book, it is possible to develop these mental factors to the point where we actually realize them.

Both aspirations are crucial. Without the altruistic mind, there can be no wish for enlightenment. Perhaps there can be freedom from samsara, but not enlightenment. And without the driving force of the wish to free ourselves from suffering and delusion, the mind that wishes to help others will be fairly ineffectual. No matter which method we use, however, the mind that wishes to benefit others always precedes the mind that wishes to attain enlightenment. Benefiting others as skillfully as possible is the aim, and placing ourselves on the path to becoming enlightened is the means of realizing that aim.

Consider the work of charity workers overseas. First they develop the sincere, altruistic wish to help people in that particular country. Next, they set about doing whatever is needed to help them: saving for airfares, contacting embassies, collecting food and other supplies, and so forth.

In our case, we, too, must first have the wish to benefit others. Of course, anything we do to help others is positive, but we will also see upon investigation that we are limited until we have developed our own potential to its maximum—in other words, until we have achieved full enlightenment.

Khunu Rinpoche says:

> What is the use of working to grow a shoot if
> You are without a seed? What is the use
> Of working to obtain complete buddhahood
> If you are without bodhichitta?[15]

In this sense, it is almost as though enlightenment were a natural consequence of bodhichitta. While we have the aspiration to bring benefit to others, we find that nothing except the attainment of bodhichitta and final enlightenment will take us beyond partially helping a limited number of beings. At some point, we come to understand that while we may feel pleased if we are able to give a beggar on the street our spare change, we are now concerned with ending that person's begging entirely. As we look ever deeper into the true situation of all beings, we see that we need even more profound methods of actually relieving all beings of all suffering. At such a deep level, the only tool is a mind totally free from the ignorance and delusion that now plague us. That is the second aspiration, to have a mind completely free from confusion and ignorance—to have enlightenment to an extent—so we can best help all beings completely.

When both aspirations are in their nascent stage, the altruistic desire may occur spontaneously, while the wish for enlightenment may be generated only with effort. At that stage what the practitioner experiences is called *contrived* bodhichitta, contrived in the sense that the mind of enlightenment exists strongly during the meditation session, but is lost when the practitioner comes out of the session. When both occur spontaneously, that is called real or *uncontrived* bodhichitta.

Thus, bodhichitta is a considered to be one central mind accompanied by two mental factors. This is reflected in the definition given by the sixteenth-century Gelugpa scholar, Panchen Sonam Drakpa:

> [Bodhichitta is] a special main mental consciousness [main mind] which is the entrance of the Mahayana path, and which for the sake of others looks to complete enlightenment and shares the similarities with the wish which is its associate.[16]

Any mental event has one (and only one) main mind, and various mental factors, including what are called the *five always-present mental factors*.[17] These are contact, discernment, feeling, intention, and attention. Every definition of bodhichitta defines it as a main mind accompanied by two mental factors, the intention to benefit all other beings and the intention to attain enlightenment for their sake. When these two intentions arise spontaneously in the main mind, it is bodhichitta.

The Seven Points of Cause and Effect

Just as it is impossible to jump from kindergarten to a college degree in one step, it is impossible to develop the mind of bodhichitta instantly from the self-cherishing, deluded mind we currently possess. These stages differ accordingly. Depending on whether the mind tends more toward the intuitive or the intellectual, these stages might vary somewhat. Two main methods of cultivating bodhichitta were developed: the *seven points of cause and effect* and *equalizing and exchanging oneself with others*—the former taking a more emotional approach and the latter a more intellectual one. As I have said, later Tibetan masters have added a third method, which is the combination of these first two.

The *seven points of cause and effect* method is aimed more at people who are able to understand the notion that all sentient beings are very dear to them and to develop feelings from that. The seven points fit into three categories:

A: *Establishing the Basis for Developing the Aspiration to Benefit*
   All Beings
   1. recognizing beings as having been one's mothers

    2. recalling the kindness of those beings

    3. resolving to repay their kindness

B: *The Actual Method of Cultivating the Aspiration to Benefit All Beings*

    4. affectionate love

    5. compassion

    6. special intention

C: *Cultivating the Aspiration to Attain Full Enlightenment*

    7. generating the mind of enlightenment

Each point is a topic for study and analytical meditation, ultimately to be directly realized within the mindstream. The first three stages cultivate a deep feeling toward all living beings, whereas the next three train the mind to work selflessly for them. The seventh stage is actually the result of the previous six, the actual awakening mind of enlightenment.

Establishing the Basis for Developing the Aspiration to Benefit All Beings

All Beings Have Been Our Mothers

The first stage is to recognize that all beings have been our mothers at some point in time. This can only come on the basis of equanimity toward all living beings, which we have already discussed. To accept this, we need to stay very open and have a good understanding of cyclic existence, seeing the way we have had relationships not just in this life but in countless past lives, and will continue to have the same sorts of relationships in countless future lives. Only by developing a conviction that we have had an infinite number of lives can we then posit that we have had an infinite number of mothers, and from that see how kind all beings have been to us at different points in time.

This leads us to explore consciousness and its continuity. Buddhism asserts that there have been infinite past lives because the continuation of consciousness is infinite. While it is beyond the scope of this book to go into this theory, it is vital for you to understand that if you have doubts, they must be addressed before moving forward. If they are not addressed, this point, and then the other six points, will fall apart.

Some people say that belief in past and future lives is mere religious dogma—and this well might be. This is not something we need to be concerned with at this stage. Whether it is a religious belief or a scientifically "proven" fact, if it completely contradicts reality, we can happily reject it.

According to Buddhism, the mindstream is continuous, and one moment of mind is the cause of the next moment of mind. I can see that my mind at this moment is without doubt the continuation of my mind a few moments ago; today's mind is a continuation of yesterday's; and yesterday's, of the day before yesterday's, as far back as I can remember. Beyond our memory, however, what happens? It has been proved scientifically that at three months babies have consciousness and emotions. Does the mind magically start at that moment? Is it somehow created from the physical body? How far back can we trace it? Even if the different scientific theories about the beginning of the universe are correct, they are still only talking about the beginning of this present universe and not the beginning of life. His Holiness the Dalai Lama says that he has no problem when scientists talk about the Big Bang theory, but he would like to ask them *which* Big Bang.

I think it is as difficult for Western scientists to prove that life has a beginning as it is for Buddhists to prove that it doesn't. There is no clear evidence, but we have the twelve links of dependent origination[18] to clearly show the unending, cyclic nature of life, and allow us to accept that is to accept that life *is* beginningless. Anything I experience now is a result of something—it has a cause—and that applies to my current body. My body now might be the result of the joining of my parents' sperm and egg, but what was the cause of that? If you have some conviction in karma, then trying to determine an absolute start-point is futile. The chains of cause and result go on back into infinity.

It is not necessary to determine that *this* particular being was my mother at *that* time in *that* way, but only that there cannot be a being who has not been my mother, and that, in general, to have given birth to me and raised me was to have shown incredible kindness.

Why is this first step so important? If we are indifferent to some-body, it is difficult to have a mind wishing to help them. That is nat-ural. On the other hand, if we have a connection, then it is easy to do something. And the closer we feel to a person, the stronger the wish to help.

For example, although my mother lived three thousand miles away, and although there were many women in London the same age who were in great difficulty, when I received word that my mother was dying, I dropped everything and flew back to be with her. There was no question. I felt closer to her simply because she was my mother.

We generate closer feelings toward our mothers than any other being. And this feeling of love, affection, and kindness that arises so spontaneously toward our mother is just the kind of feeling we need to develop toward all living beings. By bringing to mind the feeling we have for our mother, and then seeing that all beings have been our mothers, it is possible to transfer that love and affection to all beings.

Many great Kadampa masters have considered this to be one of the most difficult points in the whole of the lamrim teachings (the grad-ual path to enlightenment). However, no matter which technique we use to develop bodhichitta, we have to follow a method that will cul-tivate the mind that cares equally for all beings. This technique is the most skillful and effective method. Once we have some conviction that all beings have really been our mothers, we are able to transcend the issue of whether they have actually been kind to us and practice compassion.

Recalling the Kindness of Others

"All beings have been my mother at one time or another, and because of that all beings have been incredibly kind to me." This is the second line of reasoning. Some may question why the mother is identified in this maxim. In general, mother and child share a natural bond, and between two parents the mother generally accepts the caring role. Whether it is instinct or not, there is that wish to take care of the child. The vast majority of those billions of mothers on the planet today have a sincere feeling that is unconditional and very caring, where they willingly take responsibility for the lives of their children.

Perhaps your parents were not perfect parents—they may even have beaten and mistreated you—but you wouldn't be alive without them. The fact that you have reached this stage of your development means they have certainly shown you great kindness in one way or another. We are alive and thriving because of the care they showed us when we were at our most vulnerable stage. Our mothers shared their bodies with us for nine months, risking their own lives just so that we might be here today.

That is why using the mother as the object is the strongest line of reasoning. One could try to reason that we have close relationships with good friends, but if we investigate we will see that very few friendships are unconditional. There is nothing wrong with using friends for this meditation, but, for me, using mothers makes more sense because I can meditate on how they have benefited me over countless lives. There is something stronger here than any friendship. Nagarjuna says:

> The amount of milk we have drunk from our mothers is greater than the amount of water in the oceans.[19]

Of course, mothers are the prime examples of the kindness of others, but we can also look at what people all around us are continually doing for us. From the moment we entered our mother's womb to the moment an undertaker lays us in a coffin, every aspect of our lives has been utterly dependent on others, and whether they have been consciously kind or not, the kindness that is present in their actions is all that keeps us alive.

Even when we leave home and become "independent," we are still utterly dependent on others: those who built our apartment, those who drive the buses, those who deliver the food to the supermarkets. Many of those "others" we have never met, but they hold the key to our very survival. Try making a list of all those who have allowed you to exist this day, and there wouldn't be enough paper in the world (or memory on a computer) to complete the list. Separate the motivation we impute on the actions of others from the help they actually give. Of course, it is doubtful whether the majority of beings involved in our universe are primarily concerned with our welfare, but nevertheless they are vital for our survival and happiness, and as such are infinitely kind.

If this seems like a bit of a mind-game, please remember the huge goal we are working toward: we want to develop the completely open mind of enlightenment, the mind that seeks enlightenment in order to free all beings from suffering. Beings who have achieved this mind have done so not accidentally, but through actively developing positive qualities to their ultimate, creating all the necessary causes and conditions.

Buddhist literature states that, in terms of kindness, there is absolutely no difference between buddhas and sentient beings. Buddhas are infinitely kind in that they give us the tools we need to develop our potential, but sentient beings are equally kind in that they are the basis upon which we use those tools to develop that potential.

The Buddha Shakyamuni gave us amazing teachings for dealing with our attachment, aversion, and ignorance and for developing love, compassion, and understanding. But without sentient beings there would be no objects of that love, compassion, or understanding. The Buddha's teachings would be useless.

If we wanted to build a statue, we would need both tools and raw material. In the same way, the attainment of enlightenment requires tools (the Dharma) and raw material (sentient beings). Both are equally important, and in his great text Shantideva says:

> Thus since beings have a share
> In giving rise to supreme Buddha qualities,
> Surely it is correct to venerate them
> As they are similar in merely this respect?[20]

Some may say that to love the Buddha and disregard other sentient beings is somehow hypocritical. The sole concern of the Buddha is for the welfare of all beings. We profess to be his followers and yet have no concern for those he has concern for. We are not only ignoring his teachings, we are being disrespectful to his main ideal. A Tibetan analogy is that of the spiritual master and his beloved dog. He loves his dog and cares for it like a father does a son. On the one hand you revere your master and take his advice to heart, but on the other you despise his dog. Can you see how this would bring a degree of emotional confusion? To revere the Buddha and his teachings and yet ignore Buddhism's fundamental tenet likewise creates mental conflict.

If we profess to be the Buddha's followers and yet disregard other beings we are being disrespectful to his main ideal. Furthermore, to actively block the suffering of others, which this would mean, would create mental conflict within ourselves, and ultimately defeat our purpose of spiritual advancement.

Resolving to Repay the Kindness

If each sentient being has been our parent and has done incredibly kind things for us, then it is natural that we would want to repay that kindness in some way.

Although there is absolutely no difference between myself and others insofar as we all don't want suffering and do want happiness, there is a profound difference in numbers. I am one; others are countless. Therefore my needs and my sufferings are utterly insignificant compared to those of the masses. As His Holiness the Dalai Lama says,

> No matter how important an individual is, the interest of that individual is the interest of only one being, whereas the interest of others is the interest of an infinite number of beings.[21]

When it is one—"I"—even if life becomes an utter disaster, it's just one person's life going badly. It's sad, but there are much worse things that could happen. When we look at the suffering of others, we are talking not about hundreds or thousands but billions and billions. If we want to develop spiritually, then we naturally need to focus on the greater good. That instinct to place the "I" at the center is so limiting.

If you contemplate for just a little while how insignificant we as individuals are compared to all others, you will notice how the ego brings up a million well-reasoned arguments about why *my* suffering is more important than *theirs*. In may seem impossible that we could ever think of others as anything equal to or more important than ourselves.

In fact, we may see the majority of others as obstacles to our well-being and survival, competitors for a slice of the pie that is life. This is absolutely not true. They are vital to our well-being and survival, and are the source of all our happiness.

Given that, it is natural we should want to repay that kindness, and the best way is with the mind that wants to attain enlightenment. In his *Lamrim Chenmo*, when asked how we can repay beings' kindness, Lama Tsongkhapa says:

> No matter how much wealth and happiness your mothers obtain in cyclic existence, it deceives them. You must repay their kindness, thinking, "Previously, my mothers were seriously wounded because of the afflictions that maddened them. On top of that, I have inflicted further sufferings on those who were already so grievously suffering, like rubbing salt in their open wounds. Now I will [redress that] by establishing these [kind mother] sentient beings, who have previously helped me so much, in the bliss of liberation, nirvana."[22]

From my own experience, I have found it is very useful here to remember the second topic in the lamrim, the precious human rebirth. There are six and a half billion human beings on this planet and they all have been very kind to me, but within that huge number only a tiny percentage have any idea about developing a good heart. I, however, have all of these capabilities, all of these chances, and all of this support. If I really want to repay the kindness of others, this is the time.

Whether I attain enlightenment or not, my main motivation is to help others. That is my wish, but of course so many circumstances and mental habits act as obstacles. If we are intent on developing the altruistic mind, then while the motivation to achieve enlightenment must be with us in everything we do, the end product is not the sole reason for our actions. The process itself—the actual help we bring others—is also a reason for doing what we are doing. I can ultimately help all beings by getting enlightened, but I get enlightened by helping as many beings as I can, on as vast a scale as I am able.

Lama Tsongkhapa says:

Therefore, in order to have affection for all living beings, cultivate the view that they are [all] as close to you as your friends and relatives. Since your mother is the person dearest to you, cultivate the sense that all living beings are your mothers. Furthermore, recollect the great kindness they have shown you as your mothers and so cultivate the wish to repay that kindness. From these initial three steps on how to cherish all beings, the result is a love for all living beings like a mother for her only child. From this love arises compassion.[23]

THE ACTUAL METHOD OF CULTIVATING THE ASPIRATION TO BENEFIT ALL BEINGS

The Cultivation of Affectionate Love

There are two aspects to the cultivation of affectionate love. First, a strong feeling of closeness is developed toward all living beings—the three steps just discussed. Then, based on those advancements, we develop the strong wish that all living beings have happiness and the causes of happiness.

While the previous section demonstrated the fixed sequence of events involved in the cultivation of closeness to all beings, the first two aspect of cultivating the aspiration to benefit other beings—love and compassion—has no set sequence. It wholly depends on whichever aspect we approach first. If we are drawn toward seeing how all beings desire genuine, long-lasting happiness and its causes but completely lack it, then we begin this phase of our training with love. If, on the other hand, it is the suffering of others that motivates us to develop the altruistic mind, then we start with compassion.

Perhaps we should discuss exactly what love is, and who we should love. From a Buddhist point of view, love is simply the wish that someone be happy, nothing more. In this exercise we aim to develop love for all living beings, nothing less. If we have reached this stage in the training, then we already feel a deep sense of closeness toward all beings. We can now consider them all and generate the wish for them to gain genuine, long-lasting happiness and its causes.

Happiness has many different degrees. For someone lacking friendship, finding people to share feelings with brings a sense of joy and fulfillment. This is happiness to that person, but we can see quite easily that it is temporary and partial. Of course, temporary happiness is important in our lives at this moment—after all, this is what the majority of us spend the majority of our time trying to acquire. But here we are dedicated to pursuing a happiness that is utterly devoid of any kind of suffering, even the potential for suffering. This can only come about through the complete cessation of all levels of suffering within the mindstream. When we completely eliminate ignorance at its root, that cessation brings genuine long-lasting happiness. We *must* include that when we meditate on love. And so the *what* of our meditation is huge, as is the *who*, each and every sentient being.

If you are used to reciting the long *four immeasurables* prayer, then you will already know the process for developing affectionate love. We start with the thought that it would be nice: "How nice it would be if all sentient beings had happiness and its causes."

Then we make that wish stronger: "May they have happiness and its causes."

And finally, we bring ourselves into the equation. "*I* will cause them to have happiness and its causes." Lama Zopa Rinpoche strengthens this last wish further by adding "by myself alone." With this last aspiration we move from the mere wish that all sentient beings have happiness and its causes to the next step—that we ourselves *alone* will take the responsibility to bring them that happiness.

Although our main goal is the cultivation of a mind that genuinely wishes all beings to have complete happiness, and to take personal responsibility to bring this about, when it comes to the actual training, instead of taking *all* living beings, we choose a particular person or group of people and focus on them initially. It makes sense to make this our friend and to train our mind to connect with that person, thinking, "How nice it would be if he or she were happy," "May he or she be happy," "I will cause him or her to be happy." *All sentient beings* is just too general an object, and our meditation could easily collapse if we tried to encompass the whole of the universe in our love at this stage, so it is good to begin within limits that work for us and then slowly expand out. On this subject, Lama Tsongkhapa says:

> Following his discourse on wisdom, Kamalashila laid out the method to gradually develop equanimity, love, and compassion while at the same time distinguishing specific objects of meditation. This is an extremely important point. If you train in the methods of equanimity, love, and compassion using only a general object of meditation from the beginning rather than a specific one, you will only seem to generate these qualities, but when you try to apply them to specific beings you will be unsuccessful. However, by cultivating such attitudes in your meditation toward one person, as I have explained, you can gradually increase the number of beings you visualize until you can ultimately take all beings as your object of meditation.[24]

Continual repetition will bring familiarity, and familiarity will strengthen our minds, not dull them. Over and over again, we need to meditate on the first point—Wouldn't it be nice if they were happy; and then over and over on the second—May they be happy; and over and over on the third—I will cause them to be happy. As we contemplate their futile quest for happiness, love will grow. When we have developed some degree of affectionate love for one person or for a small group, we then expand our object of meditation to encompass more people, slowly including those who currently harm us and those we ignore, expanding and expanding until we take in all sentient beings.

Eventually no matter what sentient being appears before us, that same genuine feeling of love will arise naturally.

The Cultivation of Compassion

With this strong sense of closeness toward all living beings, it is easy to see that, while nobody ever wishes for the slightest suffering, we are all constantly at the mercy of all sorts of unwanted experiences, both major and minor. And even for those few not manifestly suffering in any way, there is always the potential for suffering. This is a mere fact of the nature of the conditioned existence in which we all live. Understanding this is the start of compassion, because along with that understanding and the empathy it engenders comes the wish that this suffering condition were not so. Just as love is the wish that someone be happy, compassion is the wish that someone be free from suffering.

As with love, the object of our compassion is all living beings without exception. The compassionate wish is not just that some beings (my friends) be free from suffering, but *all* beings. That must be very clear. It can be overwhelming when we get some sense of the scale of suffering in the world. Everywhere we look, beneath the veneer of OK-ness or even happiness, people are carrying a huge burden of potential and manifest unhappiness. If we look deeply and ask who in truth is completely happy, we will see the degree of delusion we all live under.

And yet, every living being has an equal right to be happy. This is the tragedy of life, and this is what will trigger us to actually do something about changing the situation. Ignorance is causing their suffering and trapping them, making them unable to break out of the vicious circle of cause and effect, and so *I* must somehow help them.

The strength of the compassion we cultivate therefore depends on the depth of our understanding of the levels of suffering endured by all sentient beings. The more complete our understanding of samsara, the deeper and more comprehensive our compassion for all beings will be.

Lama Tsongkhapa divides his *Lamrim Chenmo* into three "scopes," or levels of understanding. The lower scope involves the practices that bring about a better rebirth, the medium scope involves the practices that will free us from cyclic existence, and the great scope involves the practices that will bring about full enlightenment in order to free all others from cyclic existence.

The actual technique for cultivating compassion is similar to that for cultivating love, with the same three stages of meditation. We initially contemplate a world without suffering. We then move to wish a cessation of suffering for all living beings. And finally, we take personal responsibility for the cessation of others' suffering, repeating "I myself, alone, will cause them to be free from all kinds of suffering."

As with the actual meditation on love, it is helpful to start with a particular person or group and apply each of these three stages, and then move to bigger and bigger groups of beings until we encompass all living beings.

Our final goal is to feel compassion toward all living beings, but to make the training real for us, we have to use beings we already have a strong connection with and then slowly extend our range. Lama Tsongkhapa advises us:

> The way to develop compassion is as follows. Consider how all your kind mother sentient beings have fallen into samsara and are experiencing all kinds of general and specific suffering, as

I have already explained. If you have already developed an understanding of your own general and specific suffering by training in the path of the person of the medium scope, and if through that you thoroughly know your own situation, you will then be able to develop compassion for others easily. Considering your own suffering develops the determination to be free; considering the suffering of others develops compassion. Without considering your own suffering first, however, you will be unable to achieve this vital point.[25]

Special Intention

Developing special intention, the sixth point, takes love and compassion to the extent that we determine to really take responsibility for others and to actually help in some way. With love and compassion we have made the strong determination to take personal responsibility for all beings; with special intention we actually do something about it. It's like standing on the edge of a swimming pool full of icy water. Love and compassion is the decision to jump, and special intention is the jump itself. (I should add that you should imagine it's a really hot day, so though the decision is a bit daunting, the result is wonderful!)

We see the situation of all other beings and we instinctively do whatever is necessary to help them, taking the entire responsibility onto our own shoulders. At this very advanced stage, the first of the two aspirations of the awakening mind—the aspiration to help others—occurs naturally and spontaneously, but the second—the aspiration to attain enlightenment in order to achieve this—still does not. While meditating on what can be done to help others, the practitioner sees that enlightenment is the only way. The second intention is fully there in the meditation session, but out of session it still exists only conceptually. Therefore, the mind of bodhichitta at this stage is called *contrived bodhichitta*.

Cultivating the Aspiration to Attain Full Enlightenment

The first three of the seven points allowed us to develop a deep closeness to all beings, and from the next three we have developed the strong wish to benefit them. Although we might possess the vast mind that wishes to bring about the complete cessation of all suffering for all sentient beings, we still need to develop the skills to accomplish the full measure. This is the process of cultivating the aspiration to attain full enlightenment.

The qualities and skills needed to benefit beings in such a complete, all-inclusive way are also vast; they are, in short, the attributes of a buddha. So it is very useful at this stage to really understand the essence of a buddha's body, speech, and mind, as well as his or her enlightened activities.

If we have been developing our minds systematically through the trainings outlined in the lamrim teachings, then one of the earliest trainings would have been taking refuge in the Buddha, the Dharma, and the Sangha. To take refuge in the Buddha we need to know what we are taking refuge in, and that entails really understanding the incalculable qualities of the Buddha. Moreover, in so doing we come to understand that we too have the potential to attain those qualities.

Likewise, in this last stage of actually attaining the mind of enlightenment, we fully understand the qualities of an enlightened mind and understand that we have the ability to actualize those qualities. We are striving for the ability to free all beings not only from short-term suffering, but also from all long-term suffering, effectively leading them to liberation. Therefore we ourselves need to possess all those qualities we have seen in the Buddha. Seeing this, we then do everything necessary to become a buddha.

The Result

> The speed of bodhichitta is the lightning flash.
> The depth of bodhichitta is the ocean depth.
> The limit of bodhichitta is the vault of space.
> The firmness of bodhichitta is the axial mountain.[26]

The actual attainment of bodhichitta is considered the seventh of the seven points of cause and effect, but in fact it is not a *cause* but the *result* of the previous six steps, occurring naturally when we have completed the other steps.

When the two aspirations occur simultaneously and are uncontrived and effortless, at that moment our mind becomes genuine bodhichitta, and we become a bodhisattva, entering into the bodhisattva's path. From that very moment all our activities of body, speech, and mind become incredibly meaningful, and whatever we do becomes a cause for the attainment of complete enlightenment. Of this Shantideva says:

> From that time hence
> Even while asleep or unconcerned,
> A force of merit equal to the sky
> Will perpetually ensue.[27]

From that moment on, our mind is utterly imbued with bodhichitta, filled with the spontaneous aspiration to do whatever is necessary to free all beings from all forms of suffering. All our striving has been successful, and we are now equipped to do unlimited work for others.

Until that moment, we cannot even say we have been on the Mahayana path. This is the demarcation, when we acquire the mind of enlightenment. Lama Tsongkhapa says:

It is therefore not enough for the teachings to just be Mahayana teachings. What is crucial is that the practitioner be a
Mahayana practitioner, and moreover being a Mahayana
practitioner is purely dependent on developing the mind of
enlightenment. If you therefore only have an intellectual
understanding of bodhichitta, then you only have an intellectual understanding of what being a Mahayana practitioner is.
On the other hand, if the mind of enlightenment is complete
and perfect, then you are a complete and perfect Mahayana
practitioner. Always strive for this.[28]

That is not the end of the process, however. We possess the uncontrived, genuine mind of enlightenment, but it is undeveloped and very
fragile. We can still lose it, and although we have now attained the
complete aspiration to work fully for others, this aspiration still lacks
the strength needed for us actually to accomplish this work. Although
now we are capable of helping others on a great magnitude, our goal
is to help *all* beings to the utmost. To reach the stage where we can
actually perform such actions, we need to go from this "wishing" form
of bodhichitta to engaging bodhichitta, and then from there to the
actual behavior of the bodhisattva.

4 TURNING SELF-CHERISHING AROUND

The Rational Route to Compassion

> When you walk, walk with bodhichitta.
> When you sit, sit with bodhichitta.
> When you stand, stand with bodhichitta.
> When you sleep, sleep with bodhichitta.
>
> When you look, look with bodhichitta.
> When you eat, eat with bodhichitta.
> When you speak, speak with bodhichitta.
> When you think, think with bodhichitta.[29]

THE SECOND METHOD for developing bodhichitta is *equalizing and exchanging oneself with others*. As with the first method, there are a series of stages that we go through. They are:

+ equalizing oneself with others
+ exchanging oneself with others
+ taking and giving

There are two other steps often included after the equalizing step: looking at the disadvantages of the self-cherishing mind, and looking at the advantages of the mind cherishing others. But as these fall naturally within the broader headings, and as we have already dealt with them in previous sections, I have not included them here.

Traditionally it is said that this method is for practitioners of high capability, whereas the seven-point method is for people of low capability, but I feel these terms are misleading if taken out of context. The terms "high" and "low" capability stem from the differing approaches to the subject matter rather than from some sense of superior and inferior path.

For those comfortable with equalizing and exchanging oneself with others, the starting point involves seeing that there is no difference between oneself and all other beings, and that therefore, just as we feel naturally close to ourselves, we should also feel naturally close to all others. If, on the other hand, the suffering of others is the natural trigger to develop bodhichitta, the seven-point technique tends to work best. We all have different propensities, and different things work for different people, so "higher" and "lower" capability refers to these two propensities rather than to degrees of intelligence.

Equalizing and exchanging oneself with others uses the realization that the difference between "self" and "others" is merely a label imposed on the aggregates, and so the division between self and others is fictional. Furthermore, this second approach emphasizes that the work we do for others is done not just for their benefit, but also because it is self-defeating *not* to work for them.

If I had to say whether bodhichitta itself is emotion or intellect, I would say it is emotion. This does not mean it is without wisdom, but of the two categories, it exhibits qualities indicative of emotional response more than intellectual investigation. Therefore, developing this kind of mind emotionally seems to be more natural than first developing it intellectually and then moving toward an emotional response. Equalizing and exchanging oneself with others might be more rational and hence makes more sense to us, but the intellectual mind is a rational mind, and we need more than logic to generate bodhichitta. "Two plus two equals four" makes sense in our heads, but it does not necessarily bring any emotional involvement or sense of responsibility. Using this method, our minds could get caught up in rational explanations and fail to spur us on to the emotional involvement needed to trigger the mind of enlightenment.

By using the seven points of cause and effect, a practitioner might develop real bodhichitta yet still not have a complete understanding of emptiness. However, in equalizing and exchanging oneself with others, a practitioner must attain some understanding of emptiness before gaining bodhichitta—the technique demands that—and that understanding must be at least a very solid conceptual understanding, which is why this technique is considered highly advanced.

We naturally put the "I" at the center of our lives as the most important thing. That is perfectly normal, and society believes it is the correct way to behave. This technique of equalizing and then exchanging ourselves with others is a very skillful way of reversing that natural but harmful trait that so dominates us.

Equalizing Oneself with Others

In *A Guide to the Bodhisattva's Way of Life* Shantideva says:

> First of all I should make an effort
> To meditate upon the equality between self and others:
> I should protect all beings as I do myself
> Because we are all equal in (wanting) pleasure and
>   (not wanting) pain.

> Although there are many different parts and aspects such as
>   the hand;
> As a body that is to be protected they are one.
> Likewise all the different sentient beings in their pleasure and
>   their pain
> Have a wish to be happy that is the same as mine.[30]

The "equalizing" in equalizing and exchanging oneself with others is a type of equanimity, but it is not the same as the mind of immeasurable equanimity that I have discussed before. In some way, this mind is even more profound.

Immeasurable equanimity is the mind that is at least free from gross attachment and aversion toward all living beings, no matter how they have treated us. From our own side there is no attachment toward one group of sentient beings or hostility toward another group, nor is there neglect for those who have neither helped nor harmed us. If we are utterly free from those three emotions with regard to *all* living beings, we have achieved immeasurable equanimity.

This is the basis for the cultivation of the practice of equalizing oneself with others. Both minds are called *equanimity*, but there is a difference. Whereas immeasurable equanimity is the mind free from those three emotions but with a remaining sense of separation between the "I" and the "beings" I have equal emotions toward, equalizing oneself with others is the mind that feels there is no such separation. By this, I do not mean that there is "no separation" in the sense of there being only one entity in the universe, but in the sense that we are completely equal with others. To put it simply, immeasurable equanimity is the feeling of equal emotion regarding others; equalizing oneself with others is the feeling that there is no difference between ourselves and others.

This is a mental process; we are changing our attitude from one that naturally places our own well-being first to one that pays equal attention to ourselves and others. From taking care of ourselves to the neglect of others, we come to a state of balance in which we give the same care to others as to ourselves, because that separation of me from them is now gone. That is the kind of equalizing we are talking about here.

UNDERSTANDING SUFFERING

Until we see the depth of the ignorance and delusion in our own mindstreams, we will not be able to understand the depth of the suffering of others, and in the same way, until we have entirely eliminated that ignorance and delusion, we will not have the skill to help others do the same.

Therefore, understanding the four noble truths—particularly the first two truths, the truth of suffering and the truth of origin—is crucial to equalizing ourselves with others. When we know the depth of our own suffering and its causes, we will be able to see that all others are suffering in the same way. If we can clearly see that we ourselves are trapped in conditioned existence, controlled by our habitual tendencies, then it will be very easy to extend that concept and see that all other beings are the same. In short, to generate the mind able to see that we are completely equal with all other beings, we need to understand and deal with our own present state of mind. That is not selfishness but quite the opposite. As Lama Yeshe says:

Be wise. Treat yourself, your mind sympathetically, with loving kindness. If you are gentle with yourself, you will become gentle with others.

Is our present existence desirable or undesirable? Is it utterly free from being conditioned by external factors? If we investigate this using

the tools Buddhism hands us, we can fairly easily see that our life is conditioned and that we have no real freedom, that we experience ups and
downs without control. The future is uncertain, and this will continue
as long as we are under the sway of afflictive emotions and delusion.

If we can see that clearly for ourselves, then we can also see that of
course all other beings are in exactly the same state, and this will lead
us naturally to a sense of compassion for all other beings. If it is true
for me, then it is equally true for every living being.

The happiness we normally feel, from the Buddhist point of view,
is worldly, or more correctly *relative*, happiness. It is relative in that we
feel happy due to the reduction of certain types of difficulties. When
we take a painkiller for a strong headache and obtain relief, that feeling is not real happiness because it comes not from the causes of happiness, but merely from the reduction of suffering.

This is the case with so many things that we instinctively feel are
real happiness. For example, for most of us the idea of a holiday is intimately connected with happiness. Lying on a beach, walking in the
mountains, and so on, might be relaxing and pleasurable, but if we
examine them, for most of us it is merely the temporary absence of the
suffering of our everyday lives.

We really need to explore and acknowledge that this is so before we
can begin to understand that others also have a mixture of happiness
and sadness, and the same longing for happiness and the avoidance of
suffering. If we analyze it, we will see that there is absolutely no difference between ourselves and all others.

Some time back I went for a routine checkup, and in the hospital
waiting room there were many magazines. Most were about posh people: their big houses, their partners, and their lifestyles. People are fas-
cinated with the lives of celebrities, but look a bit deeper and you'll
see their lives are pretty much the same as ours, with similar ups and
downs. Perhaps they have beautiful partners and magnificent houses,

but a beautiful partner means more jealousy, and a bigger house with more possessions means more fear of burglars. That's how it goes.

These fluctuations we all experience may be in relation to different objects—different holidays, different partners, different jobs—but the mind concerned with them is, at a fundamental level, completely the same. On one level, the world is made up of different objects, and different emotions experienced by different people, but at a deeper level we are all going through exactly the same thing.

The Equality of All Beings

This equalization confronts us with the fact that there is no way we are in any way superior or inferior to any other living being, in either our ability or our right to experience happiness or be free from suffering. But in order to be effective, this knowledge needs to be made more experiential at this stage.

Buddhism strongly asserts this fundamental equality, but if upon exploration we were to discover that all beings were *not* equal at this deepest level, then this whole technique would fall apart. So we have to be completely sure. The texts cite three main reasons for the equality of all beings:

+ all living beings equally wish to avoid suffering
+ all living beings equally wish to have happiness
+ all living beings equally lack happiness

Furthermore, they are equal in that, for everyone:

+ the cause of suffering can be eliminated
+ the potential for complete happiness can be actualized

The first way we recognize all beings as equal is by seeing that everyone has the natural wish to avoid suffering. If we examine this thoroughly, the natural conclusion is that no matter how suffering manifests in different beings, it is still suffering, and all beings equally want freedom from it. So when we meditate on this point, we need to have a clear understanding of the root of suffering and the manifold ways it transmutes into the various sufferings we all experience.

At an even deeper level, all suffering has causes that can be eliminated, and therefore all beings are actually capable of being free from suffering. In that, too, they are all completely equal. In *Transforming the Mind* His Holiness the Dalai Lama says:

> This basic aspiration [to be free of suffering] arises in us simply by virtue of the fact that we are conscious living beings. Together with this aspiration comes a conviction that I, as an individual, have a legitimate right to fulfill my aspiration. If we accept this, then we can relate the same principle to others and we will realize that everyone else shares this basic aspiration too. Therefore, if I as an individual have the right to fulfill my aspiration, then others, too, have an equal right to fulfill theirs. It is on these grounds that one has to recognize the fundamental equality of all beings.[31]

In the same way, we need to understand that all beings are equal in having the desire for happiness. It is not only the dominant motivation for every action performed by every sentient being, but at a deeper level it is something that is achievable. Every being possesses equally the capacity to actualize complete and perfect happiness; the seed to achieve that kind of happiness is innate within us all.

The traditional texts use the term *innate* quite strategically. Normally within the Gelug tradition, the monastic tradition I trained under, *innate* refers to something that inherently exists, and therefore is a term that needs to be refuted. Here, however, *innate* suggests that it is within us at the very deepest level of our being, and as such is as close as we can get to inherent or intrinsic.

As an analogy, we can make the distinction between a man-made forest and a natural one. A man-made forest is a forest, but because it has been created by human beings you cannot say that it is natural or inherent. But then what do we mean by *natural* forest? Its existence still depends on rain, soil, and things like that, so although it is independent of human beings, it is still dependent on other things. It is the same thing here with the potential for perfect happiness: it is dependent upon causes and conditions, but it is innate insofar as it is a natural, elemental part of us.

This is a fundamental Buddhist tenet and one that makes Buddhism probably the most optimistic religion. Peel away all the layers of delusion that currently cloud our minds and what remains is a pure, unfettered mind of love and complete understanding, our buddha nature. This is absolutely realizable by each of us.

It is important to practice contemplating and meditating upon these points, eventually coming to cultivate the feeling that there is no difference whatsoever between ourselves and others in either the happiness we want, or the suffering we wish to avoid. We need to contemplate why we currently just work for our own happiness and not for that of others, and, in the same way, why we work only to dispel our own suffering and not the suffering of others.

If we take these points into deep consideration, we will see that our present selfish concern is utterly unfounded. As Shantideva said:

> When both myself and others
> Are similar in that we wish to be happy,
> What is so special about me?
> Why do I strive for my happiness alone?

And when both myself and others
Are similar in that we do not wish to suffer,
What is so special about me?
Why do I protect myself and not others?[32]

The last way in which all beings are equal is that, although they (like ourselves) strongly desire happiness and have the potential to achieve it, they lack it due to ignorance of its causes and conditions. Here, we are of course referring to long-lasting happiness, happiness that will not change due to external circumstances. As unenlightened sentient beings, we all certainly lack that kind of happiness.

The Buddha asserts that every living being has an equal right to possess happiness and to avoid suffering, but if we consider it, it's obvious that our normal disposition does not follow this pattern, and we feel that others do *not* have the same right to happiness that we have. When it comes to that last seat on the bus, it is clear that *I* have more rights to that seat than *you*. This is the mindset we need to turn around completely, diminishing selfish concern until we finally eliminate it.

We suffer; others suffer. We should work diligently to eliminate suffering simply because it is suffering, not because it is *our* suffering or *their* suffering, and we should certainly not try to eliminate our own suffering at the expense of their happiness. Similarly, we should determine to increase happiness in ourselves as well as in others simply because it is happiness, and not on the basis of who it belongs to. It should be the goal of our spiritual quest, and so we work equally toward the happiness of ourselves as well as others. Equalizing oneself with others involves this kind of training. Shantideva says:

Hence I should dispel the misery of others
Because it is suffering, just like my own.

And I should benefit others
Because they are sentient beings just like myself.[33]

Exchanging Oneself with Others

TURNING SELF-CHERISHING AROUND

The *exchanging oneself with others* part of this technique is not about turning into someone else. We don't assume another identity or become transformed into another body as in a Hollywood horror movie. We do change, and change profoundly, but it is our attitude that we change, and the "exchange" is a replacement of the concern we lavish on ourselves with a concern for others. It is turning our present attitudes, habits, behaviors, and lifestyles around completely, until there is no difference between how we act toward ourselves and how we act toward others.

And so, determined to change our present habitual mindset so that we really do cherish others (and bring ourselves happiness as a side effect), we need to find an effective method for doing this.

Having spent our entire life with a self-cherishing attitude, it can be very frightening to contemplate renouncing it. This is the mind that has continually and obsessively worked for our own happiness, and no matter how much we try to convince ourselves logically that it is a negative mind that will only make us more unhappy, it is nonetheless the only mind we know. In the same way that some people become dependent upon abusive relationships even though they logically know how damaging they are, we can *know* that the self-cherishing mind is damaging and yet still embrace it like a dear lover.

There is no easy fix for this. We are logical beings, and we need to push our logical understanding deeper and deeper until it does have some effect on the way we live. This can take a considerable amount of time.

One thing we can do is weigh both minds, the self-cherishing and the mind cherishing others, and see the difference. From beginningless time we have followed our self-cherishing mind like the followers of a dictator, working diligently at anything it throws our way. Promising happiness, all it has done is lock us in the endless round of conditioned existence. We are thirsty and it gives us salt water to drink. We want satisfaction, and it gives us only the temporary attainment of a little pleasure, which leaves us wanting more.

Even if we have been successful in business or our relationships, we still crave more. Our successes and possessions are never enough. We work incredibly hard, physically and mentally, year after year, without achieving anything like contentment, let alone long-lasting happiness. Leaving aside material success, such as the acquisition of money and possessions, or the fragile sense of security a home and relationship can bring, most of us are paupers when measured by the amount of happiness we hold in our hearts. This is the result of being enslaved by the self-cherishing mind. Shantideva says:

> Because of desiring to benefit yourself, O mind,
> All the weariness you have gone through
> Over countless past eons
> Has only succeeded in achieving misery.[34]

If we look at our daily lives, we see that most of our mental difficulties come from the self-centered mind. This narrow mind, with its narrow habits and narrow attitudes, leads us into situation after situation where only frustration and suffering result. If we are unable to turn this attitude around, we will continue to endure these difficulties, day after day, month after month, year after year, lifetime after lifetime.

If that is true, and if we have been deceived for so long by this traitor, why do we feel so frightened when we begin to discard this mind? This is due purely to the power of the long-term relationship we have had with this mind. We have no notion of the existence of the mind that cherishes others, that it is present within us all of the time. Our narrow perspective refuses to acknowledge it.

Look back over your life and see whether this is true. I would be very surprised if you couldn't remember incidents where you have spontaneously reached out for others. If you have ever helped simply for the sake of helping, without any sense of payback, then I am positive that the experience would have left your mind light, free, and above all happy. It's as simple as that. The dictator, the self-cherishing mind, promises happiness and delivers suffering; the mind cherishing others brings happiness. If a small act of selflessness can bring joy, imagine what a difference it would make to our lives if we put all our energies into developing the mind that truly cherishes others.

The ultimate benefit of such a mind is enlightenment, but even on a mundane level there are many benefits of developing a mind cherishing others. Many of our daily problems, particularly our mental anxieties and fears, diminish as we start to work for others. Cultivating the mind that really thinks of others' welfare even benefits our health. Today, we know that high blood pressure and other illnesses are often associated with anger. In his wonderful book *Transforming the Mind*, His Holiness the Dalai Lama says of a medical conference he had attended:

> One conclusion [a participating psychologist] considered almost indisputable was that there seems to be a correlation between early death, high blood pressure and heart disease on one side, and a disproportionately high use of first person pronouns ("I," "me" and "mine"). I thought this finding very

interesting. Even scientific studies seem to suggest that there is a correlation between excessive self-cherishing and damage to one's physical well-being.[35]

That our own welfare will be looked after naturally when we ignore it for the welfare of others might seem a paradox, but we are given several logical pieces of evidence that say this is indeed so. As I have said, such selfless states of mind directly attack our own attachment, aversion, and ignorance, and so by reducing our own delusions, automatically assure our own welfare. If we spend an hour of our time helping others, we might find we have less time for ourselves, or if we give to a charity, there might be a bit less money left at the end of the month. Some surface difficulties may arise when we actively try to be less selfish, but at a deeper level, particularly at a psychological level, the benefits will not stop. Long term, they are enormous. Shantideva says:

> If I do not exchange my happiness
> For the suffering of others,
> I shall not attain the state of Buddhahood
> And even in cyclic existence shall have no joy.[36]

In some ways this stage is the turning point of our life—in fact, of all of our lives. It is the point where we turn the great juggernaut of the self around 180 degrees and no longer focus our concern on the self, but focus on all others.

Choosing to Be Selfless

We have to be realistic about how much we can achieve, both within one day, and within our lifetimes. Without adequate mental preparation, caring for others becomes a facade and the suppressed self-cherishing mind will manifest itself in some way or another. We are not to simply avoid or ignore others until we are able to fully destroy this self-cherishing attitude, but we must be careful to act skillfully, so that we may avoid the "compassion fatigue" and burnout that are so rife within the caring professions.

In the bodhisattva vows there is a particular commitment against doing something you are not prepared for, even if it is beneficial for the other person. For example, if you physically give your body before you are mentally ready, you have broken a vow. Probably none of us are at the stage where we could chop off an arm to feed a hungry animal, but even at our much more mundane level, I'm sure we have all at some time or other overreached the limits of our generosity and felt the tightening of the mind that resulted from it. That is what this vow protects us from. If giving a small coin to a beggar is all we are capable of now, then that is what we should give, not empty our wallet and afterward regret our actions. Changing the mind from cherishing the self to cherishing others is a long process, involving awareness and consideration for ourselves as well as others.

And although this is a mental training, actual altruistic actions are important too. To walk, we cannot lift both feet at the same time; to develop spiritually, we need to work on both our mental and our physical sides in tandem, developing the mind a little, and then expanding the help we bestow upon others.

And so, our work from now on is to transform the mind habituated to self-concern into one habituated to concern for others.

You can try this with a simple experiment that my teacher gave to me while I was still in the monastery. Collect two pots and a pile of pebbles. When you have a self-concerned thought, put it in the first pot. For thoughts concerned *purely* with others' welfare, put it in the second pot. For me, it was quite an eye-opener. These days you have games on your cell phone or computer, so play it that way. I'm sure you will find, like I did, that there is nothing in the "others" box at the end of the day.

Another experiment is to fluctuate between the selfish and the selfless mind deliberately and observe the results. Decide for one day to be utterly self-interested at work and act accordingly. See how much anxiety and tightness of the mind occurs, and what reactions your colleagues have toward you. Then, on another day, very consciously and deliberately do whatever you normally do, but do it purely for the sake of others. Again observe your state of mind and how others relate to you. If it's difficult to see the differences within a twenty-four-hour period, why not devote a week to each extreme of mind? Be careful here, though, that you don't lose all your friends and get fired when you're in selfish mode!

At every moment we are faced with choices, and we can choose to be selfish or selfless. In a tiny way we are imitating what the Buddha did when he was working toward his own enlightenment. Staying in the forest with the other ascetics, he experimented with different mental states to see which was the route to true happiness.

Our outlook is still too narrow to appreciate how vast the benefits of such a mind are, but what we have here and now is the opportunity to interact with other people either relatively selfishly or relatively selflessly. I'm sure that if you were to try this, your "selfish" week would be one of misery and complications, whereas your "selfless" week would be full of happiness and spontaneous joy. If that is so, why don't we all start right now to turn our attitude around slowly? Shantideva advises us:

> Whatever joy there is in this world
> All comes from desiring others to be happy,
> And whatever suffering there is in this world
> All comes from desiring myself to be happy.

But what need is there to say much more?
The childish work for their own benefit,
The Buddhas work for the benefit of others.
Just look at the difference between them![37]

We need to contemplate such statements again and again. Experiment with the differences between these two minds and come to understand the reality of the situation. I'm middle-aged and have heard this advice so many times, but it still seems so hard for me to act on that advice sometimes. It is as if we still need to be convinced of the advantages of the selfless mind. But the lack of result from all the hard work we put in over a lifetime is a sure sign that the process is wrong. Somehow our motivation is skewed. We might know this logically, but it is still very difficult to convince ourselves.

When we have firmly convinced ourselves of the need to destroy our self-centeredness, we have to skillfully go about exchanging oneself with others. Not so strangely, our self-centeredness doesn't want to be destroyed, and all sorts of obstacles will come up due to the egoistic mind reacting strongly against our ambition to change. While this will doubtless create many physical and mental obstacles, if we are skillful, we will be shown just how damaging the egoistic mind is. Rather than despair, we can grow even more determined to destroy it. We will see how true is the comparison between the self-centered mind and a chronic disease. The lamrim prayer from the Lama Chöpa (Skt: *Guru Puja*), the twice-monthly practice most Gelug centers and organizations perform, says:

This chronic disease of cherishing ourselves
Is the cause giving rise to our unsought suffering.
Perceiving this, we seek your blessings to blame, begrudge,
And destroy the monstrous demon of selfishness.[38]

Like a chronic disease, the self-centered mind will color every-thing we experience, bringing fears and anxieties and all the mental difficulties. As long as the selfish mind is present within us, genuine long-lasting happiness will never have the space to grow.

This mind and the altruistic mind are contraries in that these two states of mind cannot arise within us simultaneously. While the self-centered mind is present, the mind wishing to benefit others cannot occur.

THE POWER OF FAMILIARITY

As I have said, breaking down our attachment is not easy. It helps to remember that it was built up through the power of familiarity, and so our concern for others can also be built through familiarity. We fail to see that others are as important as ourselves only because we are con-ditioned a certain way. Shantideva says:

> Therefore, just as I have come to hold as "I"
> These drops of sperm and blood of others,
> Likewise through acquaintance
> I shall also come to regard others.

> Having thoroughly examined myself (to see
> Whether I am really working for) others (or not),
> I shall steal whatever appears on my body
> And use it for the benefit of others.[39]

It is quite clear that our physical body comes from a donation made by our parents. Our father's sperm contacting our mother's egg was the origin of our body, and neither sperm nor egg belonged to us. If the first two cells that instigated our creation are clearly the parents' and not ours, then surely when they multiply to four, they still belong to the parents. And it is the same when they in turn multiply to eight, and thirty-two, and so on. There is no single cell of our body that is inherently ours. It seems as though our limbs, torso, head, and so on, are "mine," but if we trace them back, every atom of our body comes from the first two elements, one from the mother and one from the father, and thus our body is theirs.

Because our mind and body are so intimately related, we refer to both as "I." Quite often we perceive this body as "I." We say "I'm tall," when it's our body that's tall; we say "I'm not well" when our body is unwell. We confuse our body with "I." This is the result of familiarity.

Through familiarity we have come to feel that our body is ours alone and the center of the universe. But it is our whole body that we regard in this way, and not just the torso or the head. So in that sense we are discriminating as well. Shantideva argues that if it is only through familiarity that we see the collection of our bodily parts as one whole thing, then we can expand that further to include others in the collection we call "me" or "mine."

> In the same way as the hands and so forth
> Are regarded as limbs of the body,
> Likewise why are all embodied creatures
> Not regarded as limbs of life?[40]

Although the right hand, left hand, head, kidneys, and so forth, are different things, when they are put together we form this concept of a body. The right hand will tend a wound on the left foot, despite the fact that it is not the right hand that is bleeding. In the same way, all creatures are sentient beings. Just as we don't consider one aspect of the body as separate from the whole, so with familiarity we can see all beings as part of a whole, each equally important, and not discriminate between my pain and the pain of others.

THE BLOCK OF SEEING SELF AND OTHERS AS DIFFERENT

One of the main obstacles to transforming our concern for ourselves into a concern for others is the inability to distinguish between what is *self* and what is *others*. At present we feel a crystal-clear distinction, based on the wrong perception that self and others are mutually exclusive, both intrinsically existing entities. We perceive self and others as totally unrelated and different, like a cat and a dog, and we behave accordingly.

Based on this kind of attitude, we work diligently to achieve the happiness and to eliminate the suffering of the only object that is relevant to us—ourselves—whereas we feel no need to trouble ourselves with the happiness or suffering of the object that is irrelevant to us— others. This comes directly from the deep conviction that self and others are categorically unrelated. The happiness of one is *mine* and should be achieved; the happiness of the other has nothing to do with me and can therefore be neglected.

This notion is as far from the truth as is possible to get, and in fact self and others could not be more closely connected. Without self there cannot be others; without others there cannot be self. The fault lies in our inability to recognize how self and others actually exist. In his *Lamrim Chenmo* Lama Tsongkhapa says:

> By making a categorical differentiation between people, either yourself or others, who are happy or suffering, you polarize them as blue and yellow are polarities. Thus, when you achieve your own happiness and eliminate your own suffering,

you see this as "mine" and neglect the happiness and suffering of others, thinking of this as "belonging to others."

The remedy for this is therefore not to make a categorical distinction between self and other as essentially different. Conversely, you should understand that self and other are mutually dependent. To be aware of self is to be aware of other, and to be aware of other is to be aware of self. [41]

When Nagarjuna discusses dependent opposites in his *Fundamental Wisdom of the Middle Way* (Mulamadhyamakakarika),[42] he gives three main examples:

+ here and there
+ near and far
+ self and others

Imagine we are standing at opposite corners of a room. I can truthfully say that I am here and you are there, whereas you can say exactly the same thing, even though my *here* is your *there* and vice versa.

There is no real existent *here* and *there*. My *here* only works in relationship to you, and yours only works in relationship to me, so in fact we are both right as long as we understand the causal and spatial relationship of the two of us in that room. It would be incorrect to say that *here* does not exist at all, but it only exists in relationship to other factors and in dependence upon other conditions.

Once we recognize that opposing pairs exist only in relation to their opposites, we come to see that *self* only exists in opposition to *other*. I exist and you exist—that is definite—but in some ways I only exist because you exist. If I were the only sentient being in the universe, I'm not at all sure how I would view the "I." We define ourselves by our interactions with others—by what we give to or receive from them, by what expectations are realized or frustrated by them.

This is not to say that the sense of self disappears when we go on a solitary retreat, but, without interaction with others, it becomes easier to see how much we exaggerate the importance of this sense of identity. Because of our natural egocentricity we feel that our existence is more important than it really is.

Going through this thought process in meditation, we see that "I" and "others" depend entirely on labels, with *these* labels indicating to us "I" and "here" and *those* labels indicating to us "others" and "there." Beyond these aggregates, there is nothing substantial, nothing autonomous.

If we contemplate this for even a short while, we can see how laughable it is that we are so categorical about our existence. We have a friend called John. To John, John is "I" and "self" unequivocally. That is the way John exists to John. He has friends: Linda, David, and Tashi, who are, to John, "others." If John's reasoning were valid, then Linda, David, and Tashi would also see John as "I" and "self" and see themselves as "others." The notions of "self" and "other" are utterly dependent on the subjective interpretation of the situation.

This perceived dichotomy between self and others is more than just conceptual categorizing. Our pain is very real to us, whereas the pain of others is not; we *experience* our own pain, whereas we only see or hear about others' pain. But it also has to do with the sense of "I," and as the gap between "I" and "others" narrows, the pain of our twisted ankle becomes less imperative, and someone else's broken leg becomes more imperative.

This can actually happen. In a recent teaching in Dharmasala, India,[43] His Holiness the Dalai Lama commented that while on his way to hospital suffering intense stomach pains he saw some young children, totally ragged and uncared for, and an old man, lying sick and destitute by the roadside. His Holiness said that the compassion that was aroused because of this definitely reduced his physical pain greatly.

This is important if we are going to care about others and ultimately be able to take responsibility for their suffering upon ourselves. At present, there is no energy to dispel others' suffering because we feel it has nothing to do with us. The plight of others will not touch us, nor will their happiness affect us in any way. That kind of thinking is a wrong perception and a block to our spiritual development; it is based on lack of clarity in the relationship between self and others. We *are* connected to all others in the most intimate way, and our happiness is utterly dependent on them.

In other areas we can see unobvious relationships, so we should be able to expand that understanding to include self and others. For example, it is a normal part of twenty-first-century Western life to have some sort of pension program that deducts a certain amount out of our weekly salaries. We are young, yet this money saved is going to an old person who is not us. Even if the difficulties we will face when old have nothing to do with our present young selves, we can make a direct connection in the continuum of the self now with the self then.

That thought, however, is based on seeing the self as intrinsically existent: the *real* "me" now becoming the *real* "me" in forty years' time. But actually, just as the "me" of my old age is dependent on the "me" that I am now, so the "me" that I am now is dependent on others. Why are we not encouraged to lavish as much care on others as we do on this old person we might become, if we live that long?

Once we have really come to see the interdependence of self and others, completely free from any idea of intrinsic existence, there is still a long process of familiarization, where we see that we have constantly overestimated the importance of "I" and underestimated the importance of others, and where we slowly address our wrong view.

With this practice, the concern for self will lessen and the concern for others will increase, and with it the advantages of cherishing others will start to manifest. For the first time in our countless lifetimes we will come to know true happiness.

This is the actual exchanging of self with others. There is nothing physical; it is the attitude that changes: self-cherishing is reduced until we hold all others as dearly as we currently hold the self. As our concern for others grows and our self-regard drops away, and as others replace the self as the center of our universe, physical and verbal actions will naturally change as well.

Taking and Giving

In the previous steps, especially the exchanging of oneself with others, there is a strong element of working for others, and that in itself is a form of giving. If that training is successful, we will be able to willingly sacrifice our own joy for the sake of others. Already we are both taking their suffering and giving them our happiness.

This is formalized in a meditation practice called *taking and giving* (Tib: *tong len*). The two parts of the tong-len practice relate to the two minds of love and compassion. *Tong*, giving, relates to love, the wish to cause all beings to have ultimate happiness. *Len*, taking, relates to compassion, the wish to free all beings from suffering. Although it is a simple meditation—taking the sufferings of others as we breathe in and giving our merits to them as we breathe out—it can be very effective if it is done properly.

We begin the practice by developing a strong sense of empathy with all sentient beings, without any discrimination, effectively creating a deep unease within us when we realize the extent of their suffering, and its pervasiveness. This is not unease in a negative sense, but as when a mother sees her only child ill and is utterly consumed with healing her. Emotionally, the sense of urgency is the same, but here it comes from a deep understanding of the true situation of the other beings.

Taking literally means taking others' difficulties upon oneself, acting to ease those difficulties through the power of profound compassion. The main mechanism is the generation of compassion within ourselves. Although this does not mean that we are effective in immediately reducing the difficulties and hardships of others, we are developing our own mental strength and thus making ourselves able to bear whatever difficulties might arise in our work for others.

Having achieved this stage in our contemplation, the final step comes to us quite spontaneously. When love and compassion are within us, compassionate giving and taking others' difficulties upon ourselves comes to us naturally. Like a concerned mother, the mind readily endures all levels of hardship, doing whatever is necessary to release others from suffering.

This is no minor feat, since by the time we have reached this stage we are talking about *all* other sentient beings, without any exclusion. Helping even one being is difficult, emotionally draining, and time consuming. And here we are talking about *all* sentient beings! The texts say that even some who are close to achieving bodhichitta balk at the enormity of this task ahead and back down.

However, when we have this mind of exchanging self and others, despite the problems, we will be filled with a great feeling of joy and fulfillment. Whereas previously our minds were clouded with confusion and affliction, we will now cultivate great strength and encouragement to really work for the benefit of others, using the love and compassion we generated during the previous stages. The final lamrim prayer of the Lama Chöpa says:

> And thus, perfect, pure, compassionate gurus,
> I seek your blessings that all karmic debts, obstacles,
>> and sufferings of mother beings
> May without exception ripen on me right now,

And that I may give my happiness and virtue to others
And, thereby, invest all beings in bliss.

In order to rescue all beings from the vast seas of existence,
  I seek your blessings to become adept in bodhichitta
  through a pure, selfless wish,
As well as by love and compassion conjoined with the
  visual technique of mounting giving and taking upon
  the breath.[44]

When we inhale, we visualize all sentient beings' sufferings being taken upon ourselves, and when we exhale we visualize giving them all our virtues.

There is a concern, though, that the idea of taking on *all* the suffering of *all* sentient beings is impossible to conceptualize, making the practice meaningless. As with the previous meditations on love and compassion, which started small and then expanded, it helps to do the same here. Begin with yourself as your first object of meditation. It might seem strange that you develop selflessness by bestowing love and virtue upon yourself, but this is a mind training, and skillfully applying the right method works far better than trying to overextend yourself.

THE ACTUAL MEDITATION

Begin by visualizing yourself seated opposite yourself—rather strange, I admit—and extend this by imagining your continuum: yourself this evening, tomorrow, next year, in your old age. Imagine the problems and hardships you will face in the future. Understanding that all of these future individuals are the same person, you, the meditator, take all the suffering of the future "you" upon yourself and in exchange give all your happiness.

Imagine all of your problems and negative karma issuing from the heart of the "you" in front of you, pouring out in the form of black smoke and entering your own heart with each breath in—the *taking*. As you breathe out, imagine white light from your own heart, symbolizing all of the positive qualities you possess, flowing into the "you" in front of you and filling the body with white light—the *giving*.

When you are comfortable using this on yourself, extend it to a good friend using the same technique. Imagine that your friend is sitting in front of you, and contemplate the actual problems your friend is facing at the moment. Generate compassion by considering how wonderful it would be if he or she could be free from all problems. Then, as you breathe in, the *taking* part, imagine all those problems as black smoke, pouring from your friend's heart into yourself.

Even here, we need to define "self" and its role in this stage of practice. If you imagine your friend's difficulties as black smoke filling your entire body, then it can be quite heavy, but if you see the "self" as egoistic self-concern, then the meditation takes on a different angle. Imagine all the black smoke of his or her negativities pouring into your sense of self, which is a dark, heavy, black space at your heart. Through this, the pressure on the self builds and builds until it explodes in brilliant white light. This symbolizes the way concern for others destroys egoistic self-concern.

And when you breathe out, the *giving* part, imagine giving all the good things you have—particularly your virtues—without any discrimination or exception. Here you can visualize all your good qualities as brilliant white light pouring out of your heart and into your friend's heart.

When that mind becomes strong and comfortable with this practice, you can extend it further, taking on strangers' problems and difficulties. Eventually you will progress to beings who harm you in some way, if you find yourself still distinguishing between friend, enemy, and stranger.

I must emphasize that this should not simply become a strange dreaming process. It is important to feel that your mind is really experiencing this taking and giving. If you have difficulties saying that you will give away everything you possess, it is good to start with the things that you *can* give to other sentient beings without future regret or remorse. Then, begin to give away your possessions, then your virtues, and finally everything that is of benefit to sentient beings, to all sentient beings equally.

The whole point of this practice of equalizing and exchanging oneself with others is to become a better human being. More than the "human rights" that we so often hear about, this is the right all beings (not just humans) have for real, long-lasting happiness, and complete freedom from suffering. If we have that kind of understanding and personality, then we can consider ourselves a good human being. We can learn to become that sort of person, with or without the goal of enlightenment. That is a target we can achieve, and that is something we can move toward.

The Combination of the Two Methods

Both the practices of seven points of cause and effect and equalizing and exchanging oneself with others originally came from India. Chandrakirti, Kamalashila, and Asanga wrote on the seven points of cause and effect, whereas masters such as Nagarjuna and Shantideva used equalizing and exchanging oneself with others while hardly mentioning the seven points. In a sense these were two separate lineages.

When Atisha came to Tibet, he taught both methods together.

However, there is no written record available by him combining the two methods, nor are there clear instructions from other masters such as Lama Tsongkhapa. It was only much later that teachers wrote explicitly on how the two methods could be combined.

Which of the three methods we use is our choice and depends more on its suitability to each individual practitioner than on which is superior. For many of us, both of the more traditional methods present difficulties. Perhaps starting with the seven points does not allow us to reach bodhichitta, whereas starting with equalizing does not work because it is unable to trigger the emotional commitment needed. This is where combining the two methods can be quite skillful.

In combining the two methods, there are different systems, but I will use the eleven-step method explained by Pabonka Rinpoche in *Liberation in the Palm of Your Hand*.[45] The steps that combine these two techniques are:

1. generating equanimity *(prerequisite to both methods)*
2. recognizing all beings as having been one's mother *(seven point)*
3. recollecting their kindness *(seven point)*
4. resolving to repay that kindness *(seven point)*
5. equalizing oneself with others *(equalizing and exchanging)*
6. reflecting on the disadvantages of the self-cherishing thought *(equalizing and exchanging)*
7. reflecting on the advantages of the thought cherishing others *(equalizing and exchanging)*
8. taking, involving concentration on compassion *(both methods)*
9. giving, involving concentration on love *(both methods)*
10. developing special intention *(seven point)*
11. generating the mind of enlightenment *(the result — seven point)*

How the Two Methods Combine

As you can see from the chart there are eleven steps. As we have already discussed, the first step, equanimity, is the mental quality needed no matter which method is used and is an absolutely necessary prerequisite. Then the next six steps are for the sake of developing a deep affection for all living beings, steps two through four coming from the seven-point method and steps five through seven from equalizing and exchanging oneself with others. It is interesting that with this combination method, the steps from the seven-point method precede the ones from the other method, suggesting that the seven-point technique is the gentler of the two. But as we have discussed, this all depends on the practitioner.

Step ten involves developing special intention, which, as we have seen, is more advanced than taking and giving in that here the practitioner actually takes responsibility for making the happiness of all beings happen. This comes from the seven-point method. Finally, there is the result, the attainment of the mind of enlightenment itself, bodhichitta.

This third method has quite a nice sequence. It *is* long, but for our entire life it is not too long. It might seem that the actual exchange comes quite late in the sequence, but the difference is in the love. Here it is not just the love that says how nice it would be if all sentient beings had happiness, but the love that really has the power to give something.

At present, if the building we work in were to catch fire, our first reaction would probably be to get out, and then, once safely outside, we might immediately show concern for anyone still trapped inside. Self-preservation is a very deep-rooted instinct. So far, caring for our own welfare has always been of prime importance, but it is definitely possible to change that. I was so surprised during the tsunami disaster in 2004 at the number of tales there were of selfless heroism in the face of such an awful and sudden tragedy. Human beings do have the ability to transform a mind primarily concerned with its own welfare to one primarily concerned with the welfare of others. This is the essential concept of the teachings of the awakening mind.

The Four Causes, the Four Conditions, and the Four Forces

These methods for developing the awakening mind of bodhichitta are the techniques we need to employ, but there are other factors involved that can either help or hinder our success. Texts such as Asanga's *Bodhisattva's Grounds* describe these by listing the four causes, the four conditions, and the four forces that are needed if we are really to achieve this precious mind. Rather than a step-by-step instruction, as with the seven points and exchanging self with others, these three sets of four are checklists we need to refer to in order to determine whether we have developed the qualities needed for bodhichitta. They reflect the precious opportunity we have at this moment, and they are an exhortation that we should not waste such an opportunity.

The Four Causes

The four causes are:

+ awakening to the Mahayana lineage
+ coming under the guidance of a Mahayana spiritual friend
+ being influenced by love for sentient beings
+ having the forbearance to withstand great difficulties in the service of others

Awakening to the Mahayana lineage is about awakening the mind that strongly aspires to full enlightenment. When this happens, our buddha nature, the main seed that grows into full enlightenment, starts to become active, and, with a strong wish to benefit sentient beings, the aspiration to generate the practice of the six perfections grows.

The second cause, coming under the guidance of a Mahayana spiritual friend, shows the importance of the right spiritual master. If we have a teacher to explain how to develop compassion, we have more chance of developing it. In this world there are very few Mahayana Buddhist masters, and to make a connection with one of them is a wonderful and truly unique opportunity.

The third cause is being influenced by love for sentient beings. There are two aspects here: the love that is an inspiration and influence in our lives and the people who are examples of that love. The love we feel *from* others nurtures us, and the love we feel *for* others nourishes us, creating a big influence on ourselves. But so too are those we are close to. If they shine with love, then we will be positively influenced, and they can serve as role models in our quest for enlightenment. However, we must be careful to choose wholesome, caring people to become a positive influence on our lives. It is like tending a garden: weeds can take over an untended garden, so we have to be careful. A beautifully kept garden inspires us to make the effort to keep it beautiful. In the same way, if we are trying to develop bodhichitta, being around people with good hearts can help us to develop our own altruistic tendencies.

The last cause is withstanding great difficulties in the service of others. It is necessary to become comfortable with challenging yourself when difficulties arise, not as some feat of endurance but as the only genuine way to develop bodhichitta. We need to be strong to avoid being hurt by our efforts and then sliding back into self-cherishing thoughts and actions. We should expect to meet with difficulties, but our goal is so high we must learn to overcome them.

The Four Conditions

The four conditions traditionally have lengthy names, but briefly they are:

+ being inspired by the deeds of the buddhas and the bodhisattvas
+ being inspired through exposure to Mahayana teachings
+ being determined through fear of the decline of the Mahayana teachings ·
+ being determined by seeing how rare the Mahayana teachings are in this age

Traditionally the first condition is called: *experiencing first hand or hearing accounts of the amazing powers of the buddhas and the bodhisattvas, thus leading to conviction and generation of the mind of bodhichitta.* If we are fortunate enough to encounter buddhas and bodhisattvas and see their amazing powers, of course we will be inspired to generate bodhichitta. By *powers*, we are meant to consider their incredible capacity to benefit others, and the skillful means they employ to do so.

Even if we cannot actually meet buddhas and bodhisattvas so often in our everyday lives these days, tales of their deeds can be very inspiring. For many of us, being around people like His Holiness the Dalai Lama, Lama Zopa Rinpoche, Thich Nhat Hahn, or other great beings gives us such a lift. We see the incredible benefit they offer to others through their bodhichitta, and we are inspired to try to develop bodhichitta ourselves. Merely seeing and hearing about them becomes a condition to the development of bodhichitta.

Our aspiration to generate bodhichitta can increase dramatically through exposure to the Mahayana teachings as well. This is the second condition. For some people, the texts and scriptures of the Mahayana canon are the door through which they move toward the achievement of bodhichitta. By reading, reciting, and contemplating these texts, many will start to develop bodhichitta.

We might not have had contact with buddhas or bodhisattvas, or even studied many Mahayana teachings, but another condition that can help us to generate the mind of enlightenment is an understanding that the Mahayana teachings are disappearing. If we could actually see the reality of this, I think we would all find this unbearable. We understand that the prevalence of Buddhist teachings in the East today is much less than it was a hundred years ago, and we are frightened by this rapid degeneration. Traditionally, this condition is referred to as *finding the imminent disappearance of the Mahayana unbearable.*

Even if we do not generate a conviction based on fear of the disappearance of the teachings, just seeing how rare the Mahayana teachings are can help us develop a mind of bodhichitta. Only a very few are following a spiritual path at all, and of them only a tiny percentage have actually set as their goal supreme enlightenment in order to free all sentient beings from their suffering. We are incredibly blessed to have the opportunity to engage with the teachings—something the great masters compare with the chances of seeing stars in a daytime sky. They are that rare. And so when we engage with the teachings and see how truly precious they are, the thought to help others come into contact with them will arise naturally. This is listed in the fourth condition.

THE FOUR FORCES

The four forces are:

+ the personal force
+ the force of others

+ the causal force
+ the force of applying oneself

The personal force refers to the effort we need to make and the enthusiasm we need to generate if we are to gain bodhichitta. This is a crucial factor. The force of others refers to how we are influenced by others as we are developing our awakening minds. These individuals can be our Dharma friends and teachers as well as altruistic examples in our society, figures such as Mother Theresa and Martin Luther King Jr.

The causal force refers to the imprints we receive that will help us to develop bodhichitta in the future, and this is something Tibetan people feel very comfortable with. Knowing that the teachings are much too advanced for us, or that we will never be able to keep the commitments involved, we still go to initiations and teachings in order to leave some imprints on our mental continuum with the thought that they may become our main practice in the next life when the right conditions come together.

I feel that this third force, the causal force, is the reason some people take to bodhichitta so naturally. In their previous lives they have done practices, received teachings, or have worked on developing their altruism, so that when they encounter similar circumstances in the present life, it becomes easier to develop this precious awakening mind of bodhichitta. Our capacity to learn very much depends upon factors such as our intelligence and upbringing, but also upon what imprints there are on our mental continuum.

We have probably all had that kind of experience. Mine was living in a monastery in a very interactive society. From waking until bedtime, we lived two or three monks to a room, and there were endless debates. Living in that kind of environment I could see the differences in individual capabilities and interests quite clearly. It was interesting that although we were always around great masters, many monks just did not have the disposition to gain extensive Dharma knowledge. No matter how much direction the masters gave them, these monks exhibited interests in a different direction.

On the other hand, there are many people, even without such good conditions, who naturally follow the right way, or feel a natural disposition to following the right way. There is always more involved than just education and environment, and the simple fact that we all have different emotional and intellectual propensities shows this. This has very much to do with the strength of our imprints from previous lives, or even from this life. His Holiness the Dalai Lama often jokes at the end of a Kalachakra initiation that, of the thousands of people attending, only a handful have actually received this highest of all initiations. But this is not to say that the others have wasted their time. For the rest of us, we have been creating the causes to be able to practice the Kalachakra fully in future lives, and the imprints we have created have been hugely positive. That is the causal force.

The fourth force is the force of applying oneself. This means constantly making ourselves familiar with the teachings on bodhichitta: listening to them, reading, meditating, and generally bringing them into our lives.

Of the four causes, four conditions, and four forces, the factors we develop from our own side will lead to a very stable bodhichitta. The factors that develop through dependence on others will also help to develop bodhichitta, but the resulting mind will be less stable, as our self-centeredness may still be a driving force. Educators know that learning by doing is always preferable to learning by simply hearing. Engaging in bodhichitta is better than reading about it.

Lama Tsongkhapa summarizes these three sets of four in the following way:

. . . Asanga's *Bodhisattva's Grounds* says that by depending on the four causes and the four conditions, separately or collectively, you will cultivate a strong mind of enlightenment if it comes from your own personal force or the causal force. It is not strong if it comes from the force of others or the force of applying oneself.

When you have deeply understood that the Dharma, and especially the Mahayana, is on the verge of disappearing because of these degenerate times, you will understand how rare it is to develop the mind of enlightenment. Always rely on an excellent spiritual friend, make every effort to practice the Dharma through studying, meditating, and so on, and sow the seeds of enlightenment in the depths of your heart, not through the will of others, not through relying on others, not through blind habit, but through your own strength. This is the basis of all the bodhisattva's deeds.[46]

5 ENHANCING THE AWAKENING MIND

Aspiring and Engaging Bodhichitta

In brief, the Awakening Mind
Should be understood to be of two types;
The mind that aspires to awaken

And the mind that ventures to do so.
As is understood by the distinction
Between aspiring to go and (actually) going.
So the wise understand in turn
The distinction between these two.[47]

WE BECOME A BODHISATTVA when we hold the mind of bodhichitta
effortlessly and continuously. Even in the initial part of the seventh
stage of the seven-point method, where special intention becomes the
mind of bodhichitta, this mind is contrived in that it requires effort to
sustain. It is easy for us to lose it outside of the meditation session. For
the bodhisattva, however, the two aspirations (to benefit others and
to achieve enlightenment in order to benefit others) occur simultaneously and are uncontrived and effortless.

Achieving continuous, effortless bodhichitta is not, however, the final stage of the process. The mind needs to be maintained and enhanced, and there are held to be two main levels it moves through: *aspiring bodhichitta* is genuine, uncontrived bodhichitta but without the power to actually engage in the bodhisattva's activities, and *engaged bodhichitta* occurs after we have taken the bodhisattva vows, when our bodhichitta is powerful enough that we can actually perform the bodhisattva's activities, such as the six perfections. As Shantideva says, the distinction exists between the mind that aspires to awaken and the mind that ventures to awaken.

The process of becoming a bodhisattva is generally well known. Initially, we gain a genuine, uncontrived desire or aspiration for bodhichitta and thus enter the bodhisattva's path. We then continue developing that mind. When we feel prepared to take the bodhisattva vows, we have reached what is called engaged bodhichitta, whereby we commence the actual activities of a bodhisattva. This is quite clear from passages in Shantideva's *A Guide to the Bodhisattva's Way of Life* and from other texts such as *Basic Path to Awakening* (Tib: *Jangchub Shunglam*), Lama Tsongkhapa's commentary on Asanga's *Bodhisattva's Grounds*.

There is another possibility, according to a few texts, most notably Lama Tsongkhapa's *Lamrim Chenmo*. He says:

> There are some who understand the Mahayana and have a firm conviction in the Mahayana path, even without having had experiences in it. They first cultivate the mind of enlightenment and take the vows in the [bodhisattva] ceremony, and then they train in bodhichitta.[48]

I understand this passage to mean that there are some exceptional practitioners who have the ability to transcend stages effortlessly. Instead of pursuing the awakening mind through the outlined stages, they may begin with a contrived bodhichitta and then suddenly transcend to the point of engaged bodhichitta without the intervening stage of aspiring bodhichitta. When they arrive at this point, they immediately take the bodhisattva vows and, through the power of the vows and the connection they have made with the teacher, they attain engaged bodhichitta and are ready to start practicing the six perfections.

Holding Aspiring Bodhichitta with a Ritual

This explanation of the two levels of bodhichitta really refers to the genuine, spontaneous, uncontrived mind of enlightenment attained by the practitioner after training in one of the three methods already discussed. Therefore it should not be confused with the ritual performed from time to time, for instance, at the end of an initiation or teaching. Remember that many of us have received bodhisattva vows without becoming instant bodhisattvas.

Quite often we hear teachers like His Holiness the Dalai Lama give a ritual along with his presentation of the aspiring bodhichitta. Here "aspiring bodhichitta associated with a ritual," as it is called, is not actual bodhichitta but the *aspiration* to have bodhichitta. By asserting this desire, or aspiration, in front of a high lama, we are sowing the seeds to actually create genuine aspiring bodhichitta within ourselves. His Holiness always stresses the importance of having the sincere wish to attain full enlightenment in order to benefit other sentient beings during his rituals.

I first actively engaged in a bodhichitta ceremony in 1976, conducted by one of His Holiness the Dalai Lama's late tutors, Kyabje Trijang Rinpoche. The ritual was remarkable. The high throne where Rinpoche taught was beautified with even richer brocades than usual, flowers filled the gompa, and everyone brought offerings.

In Tibetan this is called *semkye chöpa*, "generating bodhichitta through offering substances," and is mainly for the purpose of making a physical and mental connection with bodhichitta, whether we make offerings or not.

Kyabje Trijang Rinpoche helped cultivate this sublime aspiration for bodhichitta by explaining to us that buddhas and bodhisattvas were present in the ritual. I actually felt that all those holy beings were there and I was being led into their presence. When we knelt and held our offerings, he told us to bring our minds to the wish of attaining enlightenment to benefit all sentient beings. Maybe moments before things were not so clear, but at that moment everyone present was focused on holding those words, and that feeling. It was very powerful.

It's possible that for most of us, the mind generated at such times is highly contrived and temporary because it occurs only at one moment with the help of a master, rather than through the gradual evolution into the fully developed mind of bodhichitta. Nonetheless, this mind is extremely helpful in the sense of really creating imprints in our mindstream, so that we may cultivate and finally achieve the actual mind of enlightenment.

The Bodhisattva Vows

Almost always, engaged bodhichitta is the result of taking the bodhisattva vows when the practitioner, who already possesses uncontrived aspiring bodhichitta, is fully prepared. It is most appropriate to obtain the bodhisattva vows from a master the first time, but they can also be taken in front of a holy object such as the Bodhgaya stupa, or by simply imagining that holy beings are present and taking them as a witness.

The taking of the bodhisattva vows is considered a crucial element in the attainment of engaged bodhichitta. Without the vows, even though the practitioner learns and tries to practice the six perfections, he or she is still not fully engaging in bodhichitta. It is only with the inclusion of the sacred vows, taken only when the person is sincerely able to make the commitment, that the bodhisattva's activities can be fully developed.

Differences Between the Three Vows

In Buddhism there are generally said to be three levels of vows: the individual liberation vows (Skt: *pratimoksha*), the bodhisattva vows, and the tantric vows. These vows are all preceded by the initial taking of refuge, the first vow crucial to Buddhist development.

The vows are listed above in the specific order they are taken, although there is some debate as to whether the individual liberation vows need to be taken before being ordained in the bodhisattva vows. Some masters interpret a passage in the standard commentary on Atisha's *Lamp of the Path to Enlightenment* to mean that one set of individual liberation vows is needed, but Lama Tsongkhapa claims that this is a misinterpretation, that only the refuge vows and the commitment to avoid the ten nonvirtues are prerequisites to the bodhisattva vows. It is my personal opinion that it would be ideal if the practitioner has also taken the individual liberation vows.

There are seven sets of individual liberation vows, depending on the religious status of the practitioners taking them. These include fully ordained monks and nuns, novice monks and nuns, probationary nuns, and laymen and laywomen. There are similar conditions for giving vows as well. For example, only fully ordained monks (including the abbot of the monastery) are able to give the fully ordained monks' vows.

In Tibetan Buddhism, the individual liberation vows last for one lifetime, so we commit to keep them until we die. If we lose the ability to adhere to our vows, except in very exceptional cases, we cannot retake them.

The bodhisattva vows do not have these stipulations. It is not necessary to take them in front of a living being, as I have said, and we can take the vows many times, even within a single day. The bodhisattva vows also continue from lifetime to lifetime, until we finally attain enlightenment.

Furthermore, we are not permitted to "research" the liberation vows by reading texts before committing to them. Strictly speaking, we must commit to the vows before engaging ourselves in deep research and contemplation of what they involve. In contrast, it is clearly stated in texts such as Asanga's *Bodhisattva's Grounds* that we must be highly familiar with the bodhisattva vows before we receive them. Only when we have studied enough and feel that we are comfortable committing to them may we take them.

Vajrayana vows may only be taken after the bodhisattva vows have been committed to, and must be taken from a living being. Again, one must commit to them before researching their complex nature.

Breaking and Restoring a Vow

The bodhisattva vows are divided into eighteen root vows and forty-six secondary vows. Attempting to decide whether a person has actually broken the root vow depends on whether he or she actually has taken the vow, which as I have said, depends on the base, aspiring bodhichitta. Many of us have "taken" the bodhisattva vows in an initiation, but I'm sure most of us would admit to not having achieved aspiring bodhichitta, so in a sense we haven't taken the initiation or the vows entailed.

This is not to say that it is a sham when we take the bodhisattva vows in an initiation with contrived bodhichitta and the help of a master. If we do that and then "break" a root vow, it may be debated whether the vow has actually been broken. However, there is no doubt there has been a secondary transgression. Vows are meant to be taken very seriously, and we should do our best not to break them.

For sixteen of the eighteen roots, four factors are necessary in order for there to be a complete break in the commitment to the vow. They are:

- not being mindful of the disadvantages inherent in the inappropriate act
- having no desire to stop the inappropriate act
- indulging in the inappropriate act with pleasure and satisfaction
- lacking any shame or conscience

The first factor, not being mindful of the disadvantages inherent in the act, means committing a downfall with no sense that it is an unwholesome action. It is necessary to know what inappropriate behavior is, so that we may recognize and avoid it. Say, for instance, we begin to praise ourselves, but then suddenly realize that it is an unwholesome thing to do. This recognition keeps us from committing a complete downfall. But if we do not see the action's unwholesomeness, then, with the other three factors, it is a complete downfall.

The second factor details the lack of restraint in committing a root downfall. We seek to not only recognize but also turn away from such negative actions. Likewise, if we find pleasure in the action, and we get a sense of satisfaction from that action, then the third factor in breaking a vow is demonstrated. And finally, if we feel no shame committing the deed, then that plays a factor in breaking the vow.

As already noted, these four factors are necessary in order for all but two of the eighteen root downfalls to be complete, and it is very important that we know them in case if we find ourselves breaking a vow. In the absence of one or more of these factors, the action is still an infringement, but it will be a bit lighter. If we regret having done it, understand the disadvantages of our past behavior, or find that we did not gain satisfaction or pleasure from it, the downfall is somewhat lighter. If, on the other hand, all four factors in breaking the vow are present, then the consequences are quite heavy.

There are two root vows, however, which do not need all four factors to be considered "broken." These include holding perverted views (such as seeing things as existing independently, or not believing in impermanence) and giving up the pledge of altruistic aspiration. All we need is simply to have such a mind and we have completely broken the vow.

There are different ways of restoring the bodhisattva vows, depending on the tradition. In one case, we simply need to fully acknowledge that we have taken part in a negative action and regret it, then generate a very strong feeling that we want to fully restore our commitment in the vow. We purify the broken vow by wishing to make it better.

After we have generated this committed desire, we make three prostrations, visualize the buddhas and the bodhisattvas in front of us, and request them to pay attention to us. Then we say our name and attend to the particular vows we have broken, all the while generating a strong regret and determination not to repeat our transgression. We can then recite either the vows we have broken or the whole list three times.

If we break a root vow and exhibit the four factors, it is important to confess our transgressions in front of four other people. However, if the four factors are not present, we may confess to a single individual who has taken the vows, and understands them fully. If there is no person to confess to, we have the option of declaring the wrongs in front of a buddha statue or during a visualization, but this is not an ideal option.

But a sincere confession does not necessarily mean there will be no negative consequences to our actions. The Tibetan word for restored is actually "blessed," and it means that once the broken vow is blessed there will be *no more* unfortunate consequences. We are able to halt any additional consequences stemming from our actions, but the laws of karma state that there will be consequences in general.

A common example is of a vase made of very precious glass. If the vase is dropped and cracked, that crack will always be there no matter how carefully mended. We are able to take the bodhisattva vows an infinite number of times, but we should never assume that a break in our commitment is a harmless matter.

The Twenty-two Types of Bodhichitta

In the *Prajnaparamita* sutras, particularly the one usually referred to as the *Twenty-five Thousand Verses*, the Buddha shows the different levels of the mind of enlightenment. Twenty-two analogies are given for how bodhichitta progresses through to enlightenment.[49] It is necessary to consider these various stages, as well as the steady consolidation that takes place once the practitioner begins to cultivate the awakening mind.

1. Ground
The first level of bodhichitta is called the *ground*, as it is the base upon which the other levels are developed, in the same way that the earth is the base upon which all crops are grown to enable the survival of all sentient beings.

2. Refined Gold
When gold is refined, the traditional texts say, it becomes utterly stable, and cannot be degraded no matter what it is subjected to: being burnt, buried, or treated with chemicals. Its pure, inherent composition will never change. In the same way, when the mind of enlightenment

reaches this stage it becomes completely established, the practitioner having realized fully the lack of inherent existence of all things (actor, action, and recipient), and there is no chance of degeneration when hardships are encountered. Therefore this level of mind is called *refined gold*.

3. Waxing Moon

As the bodhisattva's mind of enlightenment progresses in the trainings, such as the six perfections and the thirty-seven aspects of enlightenment, it is compared to the *waxing moon*, growing continually in size and brightness. The *Abhisamayalamkara* says that this mind is "all the bright dharmas increasing more and more."[50]

4. Fire

The more the bodhisattva progresses, the stronger his or her mind becomes, capable of destroying all obstacles to the attainment of full enlightenment. It is like the *fire*, easily burning away many flammable objects in its path.

5. Great Treasury

This level of mind is compared to a *great treasury*, a vast storehouse of wonderful objects of desire, open to anyone who happens upon it. By this stage the bodhisattva's generosity is so huge it encompasses the needs of all sentient beings, providing them with all they need and want.

6. Source of Jewels

When the practitioner practices the perfection of ethics, then bodhichitta is like a *source of jewels*, because, imbued with ethics, it is capable of bringing out all other good qualities, like a fountain of precious jewels.

7. Great Ocean

With the perfection of patience, bodhichitta is compared to a *great ocean*. Like the ocean, there is stillness and tranquility deep down beneath the turbulence of waves on the surface. In order to benefit living beings, bodhisattvas must undergo many hardships, but there is always peace deep down.

8. Vajra

When the practitioner has fully completed the perfection of joyous effort, then bodhichitta is like an adamantine *vajra*, a perfection that is utterly indestructible. The journey has commenced, and regardless of any obstacles that might arise, it will continue until the end.

9. King of Mountains

With the perfection of concentration, bodhichitta is totally stable and immovable, and the practitioner is never distracted from the bodhisattva's training. Thus, the awakening mind is likened to the *king of mountains*, immutable no matter what is happening around it, be it wars, storms, earthquakes, or any other elemental forces.

10. Finest Medicine

When the practitioner has completed the perfection of wisdom realizing emptiness, bodhichitta is compared to the *finest medicine*. Like the best medicine that cures all of our ailments, bodhichitta eliminates all obstacles to attaining enlightenment.

11. Wonderful Friend

A bodhisattva requires many skills, so at the next level, where the practitioner is able to practice the perfect method of working for the sake of all sentient beings, bodhichitta is compared to a *wonderful friend*, willing and able to help all beings, no matter what their specific needs are.

12. Wish-Granting Jewel

When the practitioner is able to make great prayers and accomplish the purpose of those great prayers, that level of bodhichitta is like a *wish-granting jewel*, fulfilling the purposes of the bodhisattva's prayers.

13. Sun

Bodhichitta associated with the perfection of strength is likened to the *sun*. Like the sun at harvest time, the strength of its radiance is the prime source of the ripening of crops.

14. Sweet Song of the Gandharvas

When the perfection of knowledge is reached, the bodhisattva's knowledge of the universe is complete and his or her Dharma teaching is utterly precise, correct, and in accord with the needs of sentient beings, so it is likened to the mythical *sweet song of the gandharvas*, a melodious song sung by heavenly beings that fills all hearts with joy.

15. Great King

When the practitioner is able to directly realize emptiness and the six perfections, the bodhichitta is compared to a *great king* who rules wisely, looking after his subjects' welfare with absolute certainty. At this level, the bodhisattva has not only great confidence and certainty, but also the absolute power to achieve his or her ends.

16. Storehouse

Because the bodhisattva practices accumulate merit through the first five perfections, and wisdom through the last perfection, bodhichitta at this level is called a *storehouse*, holding everything that is necessary to benefit all sentient beings.

17. Great Highway

When the great trainings, such as the thirty-seven aspects of enlightenment and the six perfections, are completed, the mind of bodhichitta is likened to a *great highway* where all types of vehicles can travel effortlessly. This being is able to help all sentient beings at all different levels of practice—those seeking individual liberation as well as those on the bodhisattva path.

18. Great Vehicle

When calm abiding is combined with special insight, the great compassion attained will assist the practitioner in avoiding the extreme of peace, whereas emptiness will help him or her avoid the extreme of samsara. This is compared to a *great vehicle* that can take him or her to the final destination, full enlightenment.

19. Spring

When the bodhisattva is able to give teachings and support others with absolutely no sense of exhaustion, bodhichitta is compared to a *spring*. In the same way that water gushes endlessly from a spring, the practitioner at this level is a continuous source of Dharma.

20. Sweet Sound

When the bodhisattva is able to teach the Dharma effortlessly to sentient beings seeking liberation or full enlightenment, this is compared to a *sweet sound*. Whatever the bodhisattva teaches is profound and elegant, like our favorite song, giving us a sense that everything is perfect. Even in summarizing the most mundane teachings, the bodhisattva still has the ability to convey the precise meaning and to help sentient beings to understand that meaning completely, attracting us to the Dharma as a sweet sound attracts and delights us.

21. River

When the bodhisattva is able to show sentient beings that full enlightenment is the goal for each of us, this is compared to a *river* where all beings flow naturally with the current toward the ocean, full enlightenment.

22. Great Cloud

At this final level of mind awareness, the bodhisattva's ability to emanate in all sorts of forms in order to benefit all sentient beings is compared to a *great cloud*. Just as a cloud brings rain, allowing seeds to grow no matter what they are, so by his or her activities, such as undertaking the twelve deeds of a buddha,[51] the bodhisattva benefits all beings no matter their situation.

It is important to remember that the mind of bodhichitta is neither definitive nor permanent. The mind must move through different levels, such as aspiring and engaged bodhichitta, or the twenty-two types of bodhichitta we have just discussed. Attaining the actual mind of enlightenment is not the final goal, but rather a major landmark along the long road to enlightenment. Far from being daunted by this fact, we should be inspired by it, for it shows that there is a clear continuum that leads from the mind we have now to the mind we will have when we finally achieve enlightenment. We are somewhere along that continuum; we are already on that road.

Maintaining and Enhancing Bodhichitta in This and Future Lifetimes

MAINTAINING AND ENHANCING BODHICHITTA IN THIS LIFETIME

Whether the mind of enlightenment has been generated through the uncontrived aspiration for bodhichitta with one of the three methods we have discussed, or whether it is contrived and generated with the help of a master in a ritual, it is a very precious mind. We should therefore do everything possible to hold on to that mind and not let it degenerate, attempting to enhance it in any way we can.

One method of stopping the mind of enlightenment from degenerating is to repeatedly recall the benefits of having such a mind. By reading about these benefits in great works such as the first chapter of Shantideva's *A Guide to the Bodhisattva's Way of Life* or in Asanga's *Bodhisattva's Grounds*, we maintain a deep sense of the importance of bodhichitta.

We can also do this by reciting one of the bodhichitta prayers regularly. This could be the short version you can find in many prayer books,[52] or a longer version, such as the one in the FPMT six-session guru yoga.[53]

Traditionally it is said we should say the refuge and bodhichitta prayer three times in the morning and three times in the evening. By simply reflecting upon the meaning while reciting them as many times as possible, we have a very powerful method for keeping and enhancing the mind of enlightenment in this lifetime.

Another safeguard against the degeneration of this great awakening mind is to keep the scope of the awakening mind always at heart, and determine never to abandon any sentient being no matter what it takes, in spite of the difficulties that will arise, in spite of the vast timescale involved, and in spite of how difficult and unthankful sentient beings can be. This takes immense courage, but if, because of certain obstacles, we begin to doubt the value of working for all sentient beings, doubt can completely wear away the bodhichitta we have generated.

We can also maintain and enhance the mind of enlightenment by making offerings to the precious objects and at holy places, being generous to people who need help, or doing purification practices. All of these practices focus on the mind of enlightenment and thus enhance it. Lama Tsongkhapa advises us:

> When you have developed the mind of enlightenment through ritual, strive to accumulate merit daily, by making offerings to the Three Jewels, and so forth, in order to increase it. Although I have not seen a scriptural source for this other than hearing it from other teachers, it is nonetheless very beneficial.[54]

Maintaining and Enhancing Bodhichitta in Future Lifetimes

The way to maintain bodhichitta in future lifetimes is to be very honest and sincere to our abbots, preceptors, and teachers, who lead us to enlightenment and are very kind to us in many different ways, such as teaching us and giving us vows. We must also be honest and sincere to all sentient beings, something that is often more difficult than we would assume. I myself have the habit of teasing people, which is quite dangerous as it can so easily be taken the wrong way.

It is also extremely important to see other people on the spiritual path as our teachers. We can't see another person's mind, and so have no way of knowing how far along the path he or she might be. Therefore we should regard everyone trying to develop spiritually as extremely important beings who possess great qualities and, without any sense of competition or jealousy, rejoice in those qualities.

Finally, we can enhance our awakening mind by always maintaining a strong determination to lead all sentient beings to enlightenment. Implanting that thought sincerely in our minds, recalling it again and again, and trying to make it the prime motivation for everything we do will maintain and enhance our bodhichitta, lifetime after lifetime.

Maintaining Bodhichitta through Mind Training

There will certainly be many problems when we initially begin to develop the awakening mind of enlightenment. Internally, the self-grasping mind, which is being severely challenged, will throw hindrances in our way. Externally, all sorts of difficulties will arise, which can damage our resolve to work for all beings if we are not strong. To counter this, the Kadampa masters, beginning with the Indian master Atisha, created a unique series of teachings on turning difficulties to our advantage. This method is generally called *mind training* or *thought transformation* (Tib: *lojong*).

The *lojong* teachings are well-discussed in the sutras as well as great Indian masters' texts, such as Nagarjuna's *Jewel Rosary*, Asanga's *Bodhisattva's Grounds*, and Shantideva's *A Guide to the Bodhisattva's Way of Life*. Later, Kadampa masters developed the thought-transformation techniques, the first famous one being set forth in Langri Thangpa's *Eight Verses on Mind Training* (see appendix). For example, one verse says:

> Even if one whom I have helped,
> Or in whom I have placed great hope,
> Gravely mistreats me in hurtful ways,
> I will train myself to view him as my sublime teacher.[55]

When we are trying to develop the mind of enlightenment, how should we react when people act in a completely contrary way and return the help we have given them with harm? This verse urges us not to be disappointed or discouraged, or feel that it is hopeless to help these people, but to see them as spiritual friends, because they give us the opportunity to develop patience through our actions and hence strengthen our bodhichitta. Rather than taking it personally, we are able to gain courage through seeing how they are blinded by ignorance and aversion, utterly insensible to the harm they are inflicting on themselves and others. *They* specifically are the ones for whom we are developing bodhichitta, more so than those not so afflicted, who thank us for our help. Being so obviously sunk in the quagmire of delusions, they are showing us how important these teachings on bodhichitta are, and as such they are our great teachers, leading us to practice the Dharma more strongly than ever.

Similarly, all of the literature on mind training is designed to turn the mind around and make us see problems as opportunities to enhance the mind of enlightenment we already possess. These beneficial practices have spread from the Kadampa lineage to all four traditions within Tibetan Buddhism.

In the Lama Chöpa, mind training is included in the beautiful long, final lamrim prayer.

> In short no matter what appearances may arise, be they good
> or bad,
> I seek your blessing to transform them into a path ever
> enhancing the two bodhichittas
> Through the practice of the five forces—the quintessence
> of the entire Dharma—
> And thus to enjoy solely a blissful mind.[56]

So we should take everything that occurs to us in our daily lives—
be it helpful, harmful, joyful, or sorrowful—and use it as a means of
enhancing our mind of enlightenment.

The five forces, or powers, identified in the verse are:

+ the power of intention
+ the power of familiarity
+ the power of the antidote
+ the power of the white seed
+ the power of prayer

Power of intention refers to our motivation. If, no matter what circumstances arise, our actions of body, speech, and mind are always
motivated by the wish to attain enlightenment for the sake of all living beings, it is an immensely powerful mind.

The second power is the power of familiarity, repeatedly familiariz-
ing the mind with the mind of enlightenment, taking advantage of
every circumstance. If we can do that, we habituate our minds to being
positive and utilizing everything that happens in a positive way.

With the power of the antidote, we hold the mind that cherishes
others as paramount. Our main obstacle to enlightenment is the self-
centered mind, and its antidote is the completely opposite mind that
holds others as dearer than ourselves. Repeatedly evoking the mind
cherishing others will enable us to contain and cultivate the positive
mind, no matter what occurs.

The power of the white seed, the fourth power, refers to the positive imprints we place in our mindstreams when we perform positive
actions and reactions. By never turning away, whatever the circumstances, and by accepting our actions, we turn our entire experience
into the path to enlightenment.

The last power is the power of prayer, which means clearly visualizing all the buddhas and bodhisattvas in front of us and then strongly

determining that we will always possess the mind of enlightenment. This is not praying as in pleading with some external god for help, but using the many wonderful prayers within the Buddhist canon to inspire our minds and increase our resolve. A classic example is the dedication prayer from Shantideva that His Holiness the Dalai Lama often states is his favorite verse:

> For as long as space endures
> And for as long as living beings remain,
> Until then may I too abide
> To dispel the misery of the world.[57]

The dedication verses used very often in Mahayana Buddhism are equally powerful in recalling the awakening mind of enlightenment. Two of the most common ones in the Tibetan tradition are:

> Due to this merit may I soon
> Attain the state of enlightenment,
> That I may be able to liberate
> All sentient beings from their suffering.

And:

> May the precious bodhi-mind
> Not yet born arise and grow.
> May that which is born have no decline,
> But increase forever more.[58]

6 THE BODHISATTVA'S ACTIVITIES

Supreme bodhichitta is the wish to remove
every flaw from every living being and to
bring about limitless good qualities in each of them.
This is outstanding even amongst the outstanding![59]

To HAVE ACHIEVED the awakening mind of enlightenment is a truly amazing accomplishment, but as we have seen the ultimate task is far from over. Without training in the bodhisattva's activities called *the six perfections* and *the four means of drawing sentient beings to the Dharma*, the mind of enlightenment lacks the stability and strength to continue on to the attainment of enlightenment. These ten trainings include all of our actions that benefit other beings, and are traditionally referred to as bodhisattva's activities.

The six perfections are trainings to develop our own minds, whereas the four means of drawing sentient beings to the Dharma are trainings to help other beings. While we can see that both sets of trainings aid us on our quest toward enlightenment, we can see the beneficial ways in which our actions help others as well.

The Six Perfections

Of the six perfections, the great master Kamalashila, in his first *Stages of Meditation*, says:

> The bodhisattvas who have thus developed the mind of enlightenment understand that without themselves being subdued they will not be able to subdue others. They therefore undergo the practice of the perfection of generosity, and so on, because without such training they will not attain enlightenment.[60]

The six perfections are:

+ generosity
+ morality
+ patience
+ joyous perseverance
+ concentration
+ wisdom

The Buddha's teachings can be separated into the divisions of method and wisdom. Generosity, morality, and patience belong to the method category, whereas wisdom obviously belongs to the wisdom category. Joyous perseverance and concentration fit in either category, as they are vital tools necessary for achieving the other perfections. Like the two separate wings of a bird, all six perfections take us to our final destination, the goal of enlightenment.

The six perfections are treated as separate subjects, but they are not discrete and should be practiced in conjunction with each other—the perfection of generosity should be practiced together with morality, with patience, with joyous effort, with concentration, and with wisdom, and so forth.[61]

The interdependence of the perfections is a very logical notion for us, when we come to think about it. Generosity does not come without effort, and part of that effort is deliberately focusing the mind on being generous—in other words, concentration. And it will remain mundane generosity until we conjoin it with the wisdom that sees it as totally lacking in inherent existence. Only then does it become a perfect Mahayana activity; only then is it a *perfection*—the perfection of generosity.

Therefore, it is important to see these six perfections not as individual practices, but as six elements of an overall practice, where method complements wisdom and wisdom complements method. Lama Tsongkhapa discusses this in his *Lamrim Chenmo*, quoting the sutra called the *Teaching of Vimalakirti*:

> What is bondage for the bodhisattvas and what is liberation? Attachment to wandering in cyclic existence without method is bondage, whereas progressing through cyclic existence with method is liberation. Attachment to wandering in cyclic existence without wisdom is bondage, whereas progressing through cyclic existence with wisdom is liberation. Wisdom not permeated with method is bondage; wisdom permeated with method is liberation. Method not permeated with wisdom is bondage; method permeated with wisdom is liberation.[62]

Lama Tsongkhapa continues to discuss the idea:

> Therefore, from the very moment you aspire to buddhahood you must depend on both method and wisdom. One alone will not be sufficient.[63]

The method side of our practice must include the wisdom that realizes emptiness, otherwise it will always be weak. On the other hand, if we simply meditate on wisdom, we can easily be led to stagnant concentration. While our concentration might become perfect, we can easily lose touch with our compassion, the sole reason we are meditating.

In tantric deity practice, for example, the practitioner visualizes manifesting as the deity from the wisdom realizing emptiness, and then the activities of that deity—purifying the material world, purifying people's negativities, and so on—are manifestations of bodhichitta.

Lama Tsongkhapa gives the example of the mother whose only child is sick. While she is looking after her child she still must carry on her other daily activities, such as making food, going to fetch water, and so on. During all these activities, however, the worry about her child is always present in her mind. In the same way, no matter what activity we do, even something as simple as giving someone a glass of water, we must always have in the back of our minds an understanding of emptiness. This is the underlying wisdom beneath our action.

It is possible to utilize both wisdom and method at the same time. We are very familiar with doing two things at once: while we are making our dinner, the problems of the day's work are there in our head, and while we are working we are thinking about what we will make for dinner that evening. For people like us, combining two activities is probably a lot easier than doing one activity purely! Therefore, while we are trying to practice morality or patience, we should try to actively combine it with wisdom.

Buddhist doctrine states that in order to become enlightened we must sooner or later go beyond conceptual thoughts and move into engaged practice. But, though there are conceptual aspects involved with practices such as generosity and patience, they are not obstacles to enlightenment. These positive conceptual thoughts are in fact vital for our spiritual progress, for they create beneficial imprints on our mindstreams. When Lama Tsongkhapa talks about abandoning conceptual thoughts, he does not intend for us to abandon positive actions just because we have not yet realized emptiness.

That is why we often speak of the wish to accumulate the *two collections* in many Buddhist prayers. These two are the collection of merit—developing the method side of the practice, and the collection of wisdom—developing an understanding of the nature of reality. It is necessary to spend some time discussing the two collections and their benefits.

THE PERFECTION OF GENEROSITY

Generosity refers to the mental state in which we are willing to give or share whatever we have without regret or stipulation. There are many objects we can be generous with: our possessions, experience, spiritual insights, protection, even the virtues we have accumulated over countless lifetimes. Generosity can manifest as either verbal actions, such as giving advice to those who need it, or physical actions, such as giving away what we own. But for the discussion here, it is principally considered a mental state.

To be truly generous, we need to have developed a state of complete nonattachment with respect to our possessions. But generosity is more than mere nonattachment. It is nonattachment conjoined with the wish to share whatever we have, based on an understanding of others' needs.

Because generosity is primarily a mental activity, the training in the perfection of generosity is considered mental training. Through contemplation we start to open our minds to others and lose emotions that grasp after our own possessions, slowly developing the ability to offer material things, spiritual help, and protection.

Our goal is to benefit all living beings with our generosity, but it is important to understand that attaining the perfection of generosity does not depend on the elimination of neediness through our actions. The mere thought of taking this goal upon ourselves leads to immediate frustration. In his *Lamrim Chenmo*, Lama Tsongkhapa says:

> Realizing the perfection of generosity does not depend on eliminating all sentient beings' poverty by giving them gifts. If that were the case, since there is still so much poverty [in the world], none of the previous conquerors could have realized the perfection of generosity.[64]

It is quite possible, however, to develop the mind that *wishes* to do this. By working to develop a mind totally free from any form of miserliness, we move closer to the ultimate goal of enlightenment.

For a Dharma practitioner, the most precious possessions are the virtues accumulated over countless lifetimes. Imagine being able to give them up freely and happily in order to help others! The motivation to do so comes through perfecting the state of generosity, and for this it is important to see the advantages of such a mind, and the disadvantages of not having such a mind. Miserliness will cause so many problems for ourselves and others, as well as make enlightenment absolutely impossible. On a mundane level, think of how miserable mean-spirited people are.

We also need to keep continually in our minds the right motivation, the awakening mind of enlightenment. Make that motivation as all-encompassing as possible: not just toward some beings, but all living beings, and not just temporary, partial happiness, but complete freedom of all beings from cyclic existence.

The Three Kinds of Generosity

The traditional texts classify generosity into three different types:

+ the generosity of giving material things
+ the generosity of giving protection
+ the generosity of giving the Dharma

The first way of giving is giving material things. From a small coin given to a beggar, to renouncing all of our material possessions, if we cling to the gift in any way, we have not opened our minds fully.

There is a general rule of thumb about what to give, and that is that long-term benefits should always be of the greatest importance. While giving sweets to your children might make them happy now, we realize that there could be serious consequences in the future. On the other hand, if we can give something that will harm someone in the short-term but help them with their long-term needs, we *should* give it. This applies to the "tough love" a mother exhibits with her child, punishing him not out of anger, but out of love. She knows that in the long term her actions will benefit him. But we must judge each action for their long- and short-term effects. If we can give something that harms its recipient in the long term, we should simply not do it. To summarize:

+ short-term harm, long-term harm—no
+ short-term help, long-term harm—no
+ short-term harm, long-term help—yes
+ short-term help, long-term help—yes

Although the recipients of our generosity are theoretically *all* living beings, in reality we have vastly different relationships with different beings. The texts thus give advice on the different ways to offer different elements to different beings. To friends, give with nonattachment. To enemies, give with love. To strangers, give with closeness. To those with good qualities, give with aspiration. To those with faults, give with compassion. To those who are inferior, give without arrogance. To those who are equal, give without competition. To those who are superior, give without jealousy. To those who are rich and happy, give without resentment. And to those who are miserable and destitute, give with deep compassion.

It is necessary to develop the insight that allows us to give appropriately, to give exactly what people need when they most need it. We should be able to give without any sense of stress. And we should not give something that has been gained through wrong livelihood, or give in a way that goes against common sense. Our facial expression should express genuine joy, and the gift should be placed gently before the recipient with dignity and respect. I myself have trouble with this one when trying to give to needy individuals in Bodhgaya. Their manner of begging is so aggressive, and their need so insatiable, that it takes a vast reserve of tolerance for me to not become irritated. A pure act of generosity can so easily be spoiled by anger; it is necessary for us to include the practice of patience with our practice of generosity.

The second way to practice generosity is to give protection to those whose lives and possessions are at risk. This can be due to manmade or natural dangers, and the protection can come in many forms. Those who are sick need protection from illness. Those mentally troubled need counseling. Those who are homeless need protection from the elements. While whatever protection we can give others is considered generosity, it is thought that the most generous protection is protection from mental afflictions.

People need things to survive, but it is important to realize that in order to really help them with their long-term needs, we need to show them how to achieve peerless happiness for themselves. This means advising them, sharing our own insights on spiritual matters, and giving them the three kinds of vows—individual liberation, bodhisattva, and tantric vows. If we can help them to live within the three trainings of morality, concentration, and wisdom, we have given them the greatest gift of all.

The Six Extraordinary Factors

It is said in the Mahayana teachings that when we practice the six perfections, from generosity to wisdom, we should enhance the mind with particular sets of minds called *the six extraordinary factors*. These are:

+ extraordinary base
+ extraordinary attitude
+ extraordinary aim
+ extraordinary view
+ extraordinary dedication
+ extraordinary purity

Extraordinary base simply refers to the mind of enlightenment itself and the fact that our practice of generosity results from such a mind, rather than a more mundane base. Generosity is a positive mind on its own, but founded on the mind that wishes to attain enlightenment for the sake of all sentient beings, the extraordinary base, it is all the more powerful. Whether the gift is big or small, with the mind of bodhichitta as the base of intention, the result is huge.

Extraordinary attitude refers to the way we offer the gift. It might be nothing more than a cup of tea, but the extraordinary attitude is the wish that the recipient get whatever it is he or she wishes for. The mind should not be limited in any way, as even a small gift that is accompanied by a vast mind will have great result for the recipient.

Of course, when we give a cup of tea to someone who is thirsty, the obvious result is that we are freeing that one from his or her thirst. But this is only a temporary help. If we couple the immediate benefit with the ultimate benefit—the wish to free them from cyclic existence—even a simple act of kindness exhibits an extraordinary aim.

Extraordinary view is the mind that realizes the ultimate nature of the action we are performing. When we engage in giving, it is extremely important to see ourselves as giver, the object, the action of giving, and the recipient of the gift, simultaneously, as phenomena utterly lacking intrinsic existence.

Having given, our action should be dedicated to the goal of attaining enlightenment for the sake of all sentient beings. It follows that the next extraordinary factor is extraordinary dedication, asserting that nothing we do is for the sake of personal satisfaction or benefit, but only for the sake of enlightenment itself.

Finally, extraordinary purity means performing our act of giving utterly free from any kind of affliction, such as attachment, jealousy, or negative pride. Any such affliction will obscure or block our attainment of enlightenment.

Although I have looked at these six extraordinary factors in the context of generosity, they apply to each individual perfection. Lama Tsongkhapa goes into great detail about the perfections with each extraordinary factor, emphasizing their specific importance and significance.

The Main Obstacles to Practicing Generosity

The practice of giving may not come to us naturally at first. This lack of familiarity is our main obstacle to the perfection of generosity. Fears and difficulties will arise simply because it is not our habit to share things. To counter that we should think to ourselves: "Up until now I have been unfamiliar with this mind of generosity, and I have not dedicated my time to this kind of practice. If I continue this, I will never learn to give to others and I will never reach my goal of enlightenment for the sake of all sentient beings. Therefore I must overcome this unfamiliarity."

We may also struggle with the fear that our own fortune will decline. Having and clinging to possessions is not the ultimate answer, for our own happiness or for the happiness of others, and we must use this logic to assure ourselves that the long-term gain is worth the short-term sacrifices. The ultimate answer is attaining enlightenment, which entails overcoming this fear.

Attachment is another obstacle, particularly to beautiful and valuable things. The best way to overcome this obstacle is to contemplate deeply the nature of impermanence, seeing that no matter how much that object or person means to us, sooner or later we will have to part.

As I have said, the six perfections are not things we practice separately, and so with the perfection of generosity the other five come to act accordingly with one another. If we are practicing generosity, then, by committing to the promise that we have made to help others, we are also practicing the *morality* of generosity. And when we face difficulties practicing that generosity, we are also practicing the *patience* of generosity.

People are often ungrateful when we help them, but if we expect anything in return for our kindness, we are not acting out of pure generosity. Whenever that feeling of annoyance or irritation arises in us, and we feel that we are not being appreciated, we need to apply patience and understand that there is no need for an overt reward at the end of a good act.

This does not come to us effortlessly, so another perfection comes into play—*joyous perseverance*. To change any habit takes effort, and we are not just talking about a begrudging effort, but one that comes from knowing how positive the action is and finding joy in it. By focusing on our primary goal, we will find the joyous perseverance needed to continue on with our practice.

None of this will happen without mindfulness and application, so the fifth perfection, *concentration*, is needed as well. And the perfection of generosity is not considered a perfection until it is also coupled with *wisdom*, the sixth perfection.

Generosity has no inherent existence; it does not exist independent of other factors. Logically, we understand that to be an act of generosity, the act itself needs a sentient being as the recipient of that generosity. It is thus dependent on that factor, as well as on many others, such as our motivation, the action itself, the object of the action, and so forth.

Generosity should be practiced not only in accordance with the understanding of emptiness, but also with bodhichitta, where there is no trace of self-interest.

When they attain nirvana, arhats and pratyekabuddhas are completely free from attachment. But that does not mean that their practice of generosity is the same as the bodhisattva's. Their motivation is different and their mental process is different. Although these great arhats who have attained nirvana have no attachment to their bodies, thoughts, belongings, or time, their practice of generosity is not *primarily* for the welfare of all other beings.

In the first chapter of *Entering into Madhyamaka* (*Madhyamakavatara*), in describing which of the six perfections is suitable for whom, Chandrakirti says that practicing generosity is particularly suitable for lay people, as it is one of the main antidotes to our attachment. This is understandable, because attachment means keeping things close to us and endlessly desiring, whereas through the practice of generosity we will learn to let go of what we consider "mine," such as our possessions and time.

The Perfection of Morality

Once the mind of enlightenment has been generated, the practitioner should train in morality or ethical discipline in order to enhance it.

This second perfection is considered a base without which it would be impossible to develop the other great qualities needed.

As with generosity, the perfection of morality is based upon our own positive actions rather than the actual elimination of the negativity that is rife in this world. While there is harm and immorality present, we will never be able to solve the world's problems or eliminate all suffering. That is simply impossible. Although we should make an attempt to eliminate external injustices, the main training of the perfection of morality is to perfect ethical discipline within ourselves, dependent on our own mind and not external circumstances. Lama Tsongkhapa says:

> Morality is the attitude that transforms your mind from one that harms others and from the sources of such harm. You should therefore attain the perfection of morality through a steady increase in your familiarity with such a mind until you finally attain it. It is not the case, however, that you attain the perfection of morality through freeing all the beings in the external world from harm. If that were the case, then, because there are still sentient beings being harmed, the previous conquerors nonsensically would not have completed the perfection of morality and would therefore not be able to guide these beings to freedom from harm.[65]

The Three Kinds of Morality

There are three categories of morality:

+ the morality of restraint from wrongdoing
+ the morality of accumulating merit
+ the morality of benefiting sentient beings

The first aspect of morality concerns refraining from any action of body, speech, and mind that could possibly harm others. These non-virtuous actions may be categorized into two types of negativities: those that are naturally negative and those that are negative due to the situation. Actions such as killing or stealing are naturally negative actions in that they apply to everybody and every circumstance without exception. Anyone who commits one of these actions—ordinary people, ordained monks or nuns, even bodhisattvas—is committing a negativity.

This list of naturally negative, or wrong, actions includes the ten nonvirtues. The first seven are physical actions: three of the body—killing, stealing, and sexual misconduct—and four of speech—lying, divisive speech, harsh words, and idle gossip. The last three are mental actions—hatred, attachment, and ignorance (or wrong view)—and serve as the motivation for the previous seven. These are considered the ten fundamental actions we must abstain from.

Certain activities, however, are not *naturally* negative but rely on circumstances to make them negative. For example, eating after noon is considered a wrong action for fully ordained monks and nuns because of the vow they have taken. It is not for most lay people, however, as they have not taken that specific vow. The practitioner who has taken the engaging bodhisattva vows has made a commitment to train in the mind of enlightenment by developing the six perfections. Not engaging in the six perfections is then considered a wrong action, not because it is naturally unethical not to engage in them, but because to fail to do so is to go against the precepts the practitioner has taken.

Therefore practicing the perfection of morality means restraint from all harmful actions, either natural or circumstantial, coupled with training in the other perfections and the six extraordinary factors.

Accumulating merit refers to the power that adherence to one's vows brings to the mind. This is also the practice of morality. A positive action such as refraining from idle gossip becomes more positive when we are aware that by not doing it we are keeping a vow. Because there is a conscious (or even unconscious) identification with a positive action, the effect on the mindstream is much stronger, and so we "accumulate" a meritorious imprint, which brings us that much closer to enlightenment.

Accumulating merit involves making sure the six perfections do not deteriorate, and further determining to master the more advanced practices that may initially seem too difficult for us.

When in the practice of any positive action, we are not overwhelmed by difficulties, but are instead able to face them without resorting to any negative action, that too is considered an accumulation of merit. It is relatively easy to be virtuous when life is easy, but it is much harder when we have a mountain of internal and external problems to overcome. To practice morality by accumulating the merit of positive actions is so much stronger under these circumstances. Difficulties will certainly arise, and we must not allow them to interfere with our activities.

The third category is the morality of benefiting sentient beings. This involves the understanding that our adherence to our vows affects others in a positive manner, and we are thus motivated to keep and maintain our commitment. When we take the eight Mahayana precepts each morning, we vow to not commit the eight wrong actions from sunrise to sunrise.[66] Our motivation is purely to benefit others, and this is real morality.

The second and third moralities are especially important for those who have taken the bodhisattva vows. As with all the perfections, pure motivation is essential to attain perfect enlightenment, as is the aim to benefit all living beings. We reach this only through the skillful means of coupling morality with the wisdom realizing emptiness.

THE PERFECTION OF PATIENCE

I think almost everyone would agree that patience is a very worthwhile virtue that makes our lives so much easier and more peaceful. Mental calmness is the result of emotional maturity, and is of unlimited value to ourselves and others. The perfection of patience is just such a mind, the mental quality that enables us to refrain from retaliating with anger or ill will at others' actions, no matter how harmful they might be. This is more than simply enduring someone else's harm while silently seething; it is enduring harm with a perfectly calm mind, one without irritation or anger.

When pain and suffering arise due to others' actions, the training in patience involves coming to understand all circumstances surrounding the issue that has occurred, and not just our emotive response to it. We must learn to accept our part in the pain we are feeling. This will come through a firm conviction in the Dharma, and through a thorough understanding of karma and the psychological theories of Buddhism.

As with the other two perfections, training in patience is not focused on external success, such as freeing all beings from the ability to inflict pain on others. Neither is it focused on distancing ourselves from all possible sources of harm. The wish to help all beings and to be free of them at the same time is clearly contradictory, as is the wish to develop patience but to be free from anything that would test our patience.

It is possible to eliminate hatred, anger, and ill will from our mindstreams. When that happens, whatever disharmony, aggression, or abuse that comes from others will be unable to unsettle us very much. In that way we can engage in the bodhisattva's deeds.

Shantideva says:

Unruly beings are as (unlimited) as space:
They cannot possibly all be overcome,
But if I overcome thoughts of anger alone
This will be equivalent to vanquishing all foes.

Where would I possibly find enough leather
With which to cover the surface of the earth?
But (wearing) leather just on the soles of my shoes
Is equivalent to covering the earth with it.

Likewise it is not possible for me
To restrain the external course of things;
But should I restrain this mind of mine
What would be the need to restrain all else?[67]

It is very helpful to contemplate the immediate as well as the long-term benefits of having patience, both of which are enormous. An elevated degree of patience will immediately bring peace and calm, which will radiate out to family, friends, and society, benefiting them and, in consequence, benefiting ourselves. Imagine what it would be like to have really perfected patience and live in a state where nothing irritates you at all, where no matter what arises, the mind remains calm and clear.

Conversely, it is also good to contemplate the shortcomings of not having patience. We can all recall one moment where we lost our patience, and made a bad situation even worse because of it. Living with anger and irritation damages not just the objects of our ire but also our own peace and health, as well as our relationships with others. It brings lack of peace, fitful sleep, and a distortion of the way we perceive the world. We have all probably experienced how even delicious food is tasteless when we are seething with anger.

In considering the immediate consequences of a lack of patience, we cannot overestimate the severity of holding on to anger over many lives. Many teachers cite anger as the greatest destroyer of our virtue and obstacle in the path to enlightenment, and say that one moment of anger can destroy eons of virtue. This might be difficult to accept, but I urge you to really contemplate the concept and its emphasis in our practice.

The Three Kinds of Patience

There are various ways of developing patience, but three are traditionally listed:

- ◆ the patience of learning to disregard harm
- ◆ the patience of learning to accept the different levels of suffering
- ◆ the patience of learning to overcome all adverse feelings through understanding the Dharma

Learning to disregard harm is fairly self-explanatory, and falls within the realm of what we would normally associate with patience. We learn to disregard harm done to us, our friends, family, or possessions, and so on, by analyzing how negative mindsets such as anger and agitation arise through the false sense that some external agent is blocking us from what we want. We want something—a career, a good time, a comfortable relationship—and through no fault of our own someone stops us from having it. We need to have the wisdom to see that the main cause for our suffering is rooted within ourselves, although others might act as the conditions that make it possible for the suffering to affect us.

Patience will grow when we contemplate the situation and see how we are not the victims of others but of our own deluded views. The harm that is inflicted upon us does not come without cause, for they, too, are victims of their own deluded views. Just as we have no reason to become angry with ourselves, there is no reason to feel angry with others.

It is natural to blame others as the cause of our frustration or pain, but when we delve deeper into any situation, we see that the cause is rarely what appears on the surface. Just as we lack full control, they lack full control. Just as we lack full responsibility, they lack full responsibility. If we consider it in this way, we will find there is no justification for feeling impatience, and we can learn to disregard whatever frustration a situation brings us.

We can also develop patience by learning to accept some of the basic levels of suffering, particularly suffering that is inevitable, like that which depends on simply having a body and mind. Our body is imperfect and therefore, whether it is working well at present or not, it is bound to be the vessel for all sorts of suffering. Similarly, our mind is controlled by afflictive emotions, and so, even though we might feel reasonably calm and contented at present, the conditions are there for dissatisfaction and mental pain. Sooner or later suffering will arise.

Suffering is unavoidable, whether we discuss petty or major illnesses, mental agitation, or frustrations caused by life being what it is. Impatience only aggravates the situation. Instead of feeling impatient, we can with skill turn that unpleasantness into a beneficial situation. This is one of the qualities of a person who wants to engage in the bodhisattva's path.

The bodhisattva's path is a difficult one for many reasons. Because it is aimed at the destruction of the selfish mind, all sorts of obstacles will arise when we earnestly try to progress upon it. The self-centered attitude that has dominated us for countless lifetimes has always sought happiness, disregarding the effect it has on others. When we start to turn that around, as for example when we practice the morality of not harming others, that means turning away from many of our usual sources of temporary happiness. The self-centered mind will react to this. Internal conflict and unpleasantness will inevitably arise until we have risen above the common egotistical mind.

Whatever problems arise in trying to turn our mind around should be seen as inevitable side effects of the destruction of the self-centered mind, and should, like the unpleasantness of strong medicine, be accepted and even welcomed as part of the path. The pains and difficulties that arise due to turning our minds around so dramatically should be seen not only as inevitable but also invaluable. When we are confronted with suffering, can we analyze it fully and see its cause? We are in the middle of the most important experiment of our lives, not dryly intellectualizing about it from a distance. Instead of feeling agitation and then developing impatience, anger, and negative emotions, we should use the difficulties we face as tools in our own learning process.

Suffering is never completely useless. Even if we can't see how it is created by our own self-centered mind, we should still see how suffering arises simply because we are instruments of karma trapped in cyclic existence. Experiencing suffering is one of the main keys to turning the mind from cyclic existence, using the unpleasant aspects of our daily experiences to help us reject it entirely.

Furthermore, we are not the only ones trapped in samsara; all other beings are likewise bounced from one unpleasant situation to another. Without a deep understanding of suffering, we are unable to appreciate the plight of others, and cannot develop the amazing mental qualities of love and compassion. None of this would be possible if we did not suffer, and so, although it is undeniably painful, it is also our most invaluable tool. There is a reason why the truth of suffering was the Buddha's very first teaching.

The third way of developing patience involves cultivating a deep and clear understanding of the Buddha's teachings and the qualities of the Three Jewels. That understanding will help us rise above agitation or anger. By recalling that our main aim is to benefit all living beings, to help them to experience a fully awakened mind, we will be able to deal with difficulties far more easily.

It is the Dharma that will take us beyond these difficulties. We need a profound understanding of why we and all others suffer, and this can be learned from the Buddha's teachings, such as the twelve links of dependent origination mentioned previously, where cause creates result in an endless cycle. Contemplation of the twelve links will help us to expand our mental horizon and see the broader picture when we are suffering, rather than narrowing our focus down to the particular pain or difficulty we are experiencing at one moment.

When we discuss the perfection of patience, we are discussing more than mundane patience. We are discussing patience practiced in the context of the bodhisattva's deeds, with aspects of the other perfections included in order to enhance it. The six extraordinary factors, when practiced in conjunction with the perfection of patience, form an essential aspect of the bodhisattva's path.

THE PERFECTION OF JOYOUS PERSEVERANCE

The perfection of joyous perseverance is crucial if we want to experience the fully awakened mind. Initially on the path of the bodhisattva, we may have many altruistic goals. But the development of joyous perseverance enables us to finally bring those goals to fruition.

When we practice joyous perseverance, engaging in virtuous activities will not bring us any sense of tiredness, boredom, or lack of confidence. Instead, we experience a deep joy that allows the mind to focus completely on that virtuous activity. With such a light and joyful mind, acting virtuously becomes easy and natural. Like a cloud in the sky that floats effortlessly on a breeze, joyous perseverance moves with very little sense of tiredness or unease. Without joyous perseverance, even simple projects will seem laborious and tiring.

As with all virtuous ventures, developing joyous perseverance will bring up many obstacles in our mind. For many lifetimes we have been chasing temporary pleasure in pursuit of what we think will lead to lasting happiness. This habit is exceptionally difficult to break. We may be determined to stay on a healthy diet, but still suffer chocolate cravings. Similarly, the "need" for what is trivial and self-destructive will persist long after we have seen logically how beneficial following virtue is, and how it is the only road to real happiness.

Procrastination is another obstacle. The mind that finds it too hard to pick up that Dharma book ("My favorite television program is on!") or determines that it is too tired to go to a Dharma center ("I have to be up early for work tomorrow!") is a serious block to developing joyous perseverance. So too is lack of self-worth: "I am so useless, I could never really become a better person." The antidote to such self-contempt is to develop a deep understanding of the buddha nature that we all possess, and see that nothing is impossible with perseverance.

It is essential to remember, and believe, that all the qualities we aspire to will come. There are very few epiphanies in Buddhism; mostly it is a gradual process of deepening our understanding until our topics of study and inquiry go beyond the intellectual to an intuitive feeling of recognition. With the important Buddhist subjects, such as the law of cause and effect, impermanence, dependent origination, and developing love and compassion, our perseverance in our studies will *definitely* move us closer and closer to activating our latent buddha potential. On the most mundane level, we will become better people and start to experience a deeper, lighter form of happiness. But within that, we will see the path clearly before us and develop the strength to follow it, despite the difficulties.

Buddhism is not an abstract philosophy; it is a manual for better living, one that will eventually lead us to enlightenment. But we still struggle to see this every day, instead becoming caught up in what Lama Yeshe called "bubblegum pleasures" of everyday life. With steadfast determination, we will grow into the kind of person we want to be, knowing that it is possible.

It helps to know that we are not at the beginning of the long path to enlightenment. Although we are not selfless yet, we have already taken steps to lead ourselves away from complete selfishness and delusion. We have begun exploring the positive minds and developing them. Perhaps we have a strong, concentrated mind, but it tends to focus on mundane objects at present; perhaps we have a great amount of compassion, but it is spoiled by a mind that is hyperactive. All of us have weaknesses and strengths. Our job now is to eliminate the weaknesses while developing the strengths. It is crucial that we maintain our happiness on the path, while at the same time persevering in our determination, moving forward constantly and gently.

This leads us to realize that while we have limitless potential, on a practical, day-to-day level, we do have our limits. I have seen many people come to Dharma teachings full of enthusiasm and determined to attain enlightenment without a moment's delay. So many of them, unfortunately, burn out quickly and may even slip away from the spiritual path entirely. Buddhism is not a sprint but a marathon; to see the whole path to enlightenment laid out before us is to see that we are in for the long haul. And so the pace of our progress is important. Take the middle way: develop the ability not to push too fast or too hard, but not to be too slow or relaxed either. Gently-but-surely will get you there.

The Three Kinds of Joyous Perseverance

There are said to be three kinds of joyous perseverance:

+ armor-like joyous perseverance

+ the joyous perseverance of cultivating the necessities for
  enlightenment
+ the joyous perseverance of working for the welfare of all
  others

Armor-like joyous perseverance means cultivating a strong determination to protect ourselves in overcoming all our obstacles. Like a soldier who girds himself with armor before facing an enemy, we need this mind to defeat the inner enemies we will face, such as lack of self-worth, impatience, discouragement, and abstraction. Just as a soldier's armor deflects whatever weapon is used against him, with joyous perseverance we will never be damaged by the difficulties that arise, either internally or externally. It is the determination to never back down or retreat while cultivating the mind of enlightenment.

The second type of joyous perseverance involves the process of gathering necessary virtues in order to cultivate the mind of enlightenment. This is the positive side of renunciation, and involves rising above the worldly mind of attachment and aversion. We can now clearly see what is needed for the attainment of enlightenment and we work tirelessly toward obtaining it.

The goal of enlightenment is to be able to work to our utmost capacity for the sake of all sentient beings. The third kind of joyous perseverance is just that, having the guts to go all the way and bring total happiness to every single sentient being in all universes. I think you'll agree that such a mind needs more than a little perseverance! As the lamrim prayer of the Lama Chöpa says:

Even if I must remain for an ocean of eons in the fiery hells of
    Avici
For the sake of even just one sentient being,
I seek your blessings to complete the perfection of joyous effort,

To strive with compassion for supreme enlightenment and not
be discouraged.[68]

We are working only toward enlightenment, and therefore every
action we take should have as its motivation the wish to bring happiness to others. In doing this, we need to cultivate strong bodhichitta,
the wisdom to realize emptiness, and finally, a joyous perseverance.
Khunu Rinpoche says:

If the mindstream is moistened with bodhichitta,
one takes joy in abandoning wrongdoing,
one takes joy in doing virtue,
and one takes joy in removing fears.

Just as someone who is famished takes joy in food,
Just as someone who is parched takes joy in drink,
Just as someone who is freezing takes joy in fire,
so do the holy ones take joy in bodhichitta.[69]

THE PERFECTIONS OF CONCENTRATION AND WISDOM

The last two perfections are concentration and wisdom. Anyone who
has studied Buddhist philosophy will know well enough the importance of both of these minds. Concentration refers to the mind with
focus and clarity, and in Mahayana Buddhism this concentration is
considered a tool, not a goal in itself. We begin by developing single-
pointed concentration, and then using it as a base, we develop bodhichitta and wisdom.

The final perfection is wisdom, and here again we must distinguish
between the wisdom realizing emptiness and the perfection of wisdom.
The wisdom realizing emptiness occurs on the path of individual

liberation, while the perfection of wisdom occurs on the bodhisattva's path, where it is coupled with bodhichitta. In both, the practice is done to eliminate the very root of samsara, but with the perfection of wisdom, the motivation is to best benefit other sentient beings.

The wisdom realizing emptiness is a vast subject and I deal with both concentration and emptiness in the fifth book of *The Foundation of Buddhist Thought* series, *Emptiness*. It is best to look to that guide for a greater analysis.

We all have the seeds of these six perfections in the actions we carry out every day. Our task now is to develop these positive qualities until they go beyond simple positive minds and become actual perfections, where each is coupled with the others, especially with the perfection of wisdom. These are the tools for the bodhisattva to bring the mind ever closer to the final mind of enlightenment.

Training in the perfection of generosity, we will develop the capacity to share completely whatever we "own"—our possessions, our virtues, and so on—without any sense of loss or attachment. We will experience the actual wish to share it, and with that huge step our goal of benefiting others becomes very practical.

Just as generosity brings benefits to both others and ourselves, so too does morality, the second perfection in which we determine to refrain from harming others in any way possible. If our own mental continuum can be utterly free from the wish to harm, we will experience the perfection of morality, and our goal to benefit others will be very profound.

The perfection of patience will enable us to help others and yet never feel irritation, anger, or ill will, no matter what circumstances arise. The perfection of joyous perseverance will enable us to overcome the internal and external obstacles we might face, allowing us to continue on our path unhindered by discouragement and distraction. The perfection of concentration will enable us to cultivate the mental basis for developing all the positive mental qualities, and the perfection of wisdom allows us to eliminate all the confusion that brings us pain and suffering, blocking us from our goal of helping others.

With these perfections cultivated within ourselves, full enlightenment can be easily attained. The first three perfections help us cultivate the method side of the practice, while the last perfection, wisdom, helps us cultivate the wisdom side. The middle two perfections help with both method and wisdom. With both "wings" activated, the practitioner can easily transcend the mundane, unenlightened state to become a fully enlightened buddha, able to benefit all living beings spontaneously.

For people who earnestly follow the bodhisattva's path, it is extremely important not to focus on just one area, such as the wisdom realizing emptiness, but to train equally in generosity, morality, patience, joyous perseverance, and concentration.

The Four Means of Drawing Sentient Beings to the Dharma

Of the ten actions of the bodhisattva, the six perfections are seen as the actions of a bodhisattva that are cultivated in order to progress toward enlightenment. The other four actions, the four means of drawing sentient beings to the Dharma, have to do with leading other sentient beings to enlightenment. They are:

+ giving
+ speaking kind words
+ teaching according to the level of the student
+ practicing what you teach

The action of giving might seem similar to the perfection of practicing generosity, but the main focus is not on our own personal development but on that of others. We can see how generosity is of great benefit to ourselves, but as part of the four means, we concentrate on the benefit it brings to others. We react to the needs of others by striving to provide for them.

The ability to communicate effectively with others is a vital part of being able to reach others and help them, whereas bad communication, even with the best intentions, has the ability to cause great harm and sadness.

The Buddha says the following about right speech:

Such speech as the Tathagata knows to be untrue, incorrect, and unbeneficial, and which is also unwelcome and disagreeable to others—such speech the Tathagata does not utter.

Such speech as the Tathagata knows to be true and correct but unbeneficial, and which is also unwelcome and disagreeable to others—such speech the Tathagata does not utter.

Such speech as the Tathagata knows to be true, correct, and beneficial, but which is unwelcome and disagreeable to others—the Tathagata knows the time to use such speech.

Such speech as the Tathagata knows to be untrue, incorrect, and unbeneficial, but which is welcome and agreeable to others—such speech the Tathagata does not utter.

Such speech as the Tathagata knows to be true and correct but unbeneficial and which is welcome and agreeable to others—such speech the Tathagata does not utter.

Such speech as the Tathagata knows to be true, correct, beneficial, and which is welcome and agreeable to others—the Tathagata knows the time to use such speech.

Why is that? Because the Tathagata has compassion for beings.[70]

Teaching according to the level of the student involves more than just giving a formal Dharma talk. Every time we advise someone or discuss philosophy or psychology with them, we are trying in some way to help them understand their situation so that they might improve themselves in some way. Everyone has different problems, mental propensities, and cultural backgrounds, so there is never one blanket answer that will satisfy everybody. Before advising someone, we should try our best to understand where they are coming from. If we provide compassionate advice without a sense of the specific needs and experiences of the seeker, the advice designed to alleviate a problem could very easily exacerbate it. This is the thrust of many counseling courses, where people are trained to listen actively to what the other person is saying (or not saying), and to empathize with them before giving any real counsel. It might be totally inappropriate to teach a dying Christian about emptiness, or instruct a child on impermanence. We need to be very skillful with our words, and very aware of their effect on the listener.

The last means of drawing sentient beings to the Dharma is the example we set—practicing what we teach. This is an extremely important one if we want to benefit others. If we are not a good example for others, then of course whatever we say will have little effect, and people will neither trust us nor agree with us. If we make it a primary aim to set a good example, then even one simple word can make a huge difference in someone else's life.

There should be no contradiction between what we say and how we live. How can anyone believe a person who tells them one thing, then does the opposite? We must reinforce the teachings and advice we give to people by living by the same principles.

These four means of drawing sentient beings to the Dharma are guidelines for people who want to benefit others on a greater scale. With a generous attitude, we will attract people. With effective communication skills, people will listen to us and understand. By understanding people's mental dispositions and giving sound advice, we can truly benefit them. And in order to do that, we need to set an example by living as we speak.

Together with the six perfections, these four skills will take us from our present state to enlightenment.

Conclusion

Cultivating the awakening mind of enlightenment within ourselves is the jewel of the Buddhist practice. Even if we have not yet managed to attain the genuine and fully developed mind of enlightenment right here and now, the mere act of cultivating it will be highly beneficial. This cultivation and practice is the true key to a meaningful life. To embark upon the path of the bodhisattva, and to devote our lives to helping others, we *actively* move ourselves toward selflessness and, ultimately, enlightenment.

Cultivating this mind means developing the strength, resources, skills, and understanding we need to benefit all living beings. If this kind of mind isn't the most precious mind possible, then what kind of mind is?

It may not be easy, because we lack familiarity with and understanding of the awakening mind, as well as enthusiasm and the right instructions. It will take time; we will face challenges. But those challenges are worth it. Enduring hardship is nothing new; we endure hardships every day for temporary pleasures and a few close friends. What we need to do now is refocus our lives so that the hardships we endure are for the sake of worthwhile goals—and the most worthwhile goal is the mind of enlightenment. If we find that we lack the conviction to progress further, we only need look to the words of Shantideva, Khunu Rinpoche, and His Holiness the Dalai Lama to find encouragement and emphasis on the worth of this amazing mind.

In Tibetan we have a saying: if the food is delicious but you don't have any teeth, simply chew with your gums. Here is the most delicious food, laid out on the table before us and ours for the asking. Here is ultimate happiness combined with the ultimate ability to help countless other beings. Perhaps we are still baby bodhisattvas and haven't yet grown the teeth to enjoy this feast fully, but we should chew it with our gums as best as we can. Nothing else in this world is as worthwhile. In fact, to my mind, nothing else in the world is worthwhile.

Appendix
Eight Verses on Mind Training

composed by Langri Tangpa (1054–93)[71]

With the wish to achieve the highest aim,
Which surpasses even a wish-fulfilling gem,
I will train myself at all times to
Cherish every sentient being as supreme.

Whenever I interact with others,
I will view myself as inferior to all;
And I will train myself
To hold others superior from the depths of my heart.

During all my activities I will probe my mind,
And as soon as affliction arises—
Since it endangers myself and others—
I will train myself to confront it directly and avert it.

When I encounter beings of unpleasant character
And those oppressed by intense negative karma and
    suffering,
As though finding a treasure of precious jewels,
I will train myself to cherish them, for they are so
    rarely found.

When others out of jealousy
Treat me wrongly with abuse and slander,
I will train to take the defeat upon myself
And offer the victory to others.

Even if one whom I have helped,
Or in whom I have placed great hope,
Gravely mistreats me in hurtful ways,
I will train myself to view him as my sublime teacher.

In brief, I will train myself to offer benefit and joy
To all my mothers, both directly and indirectly,
And respectfully take upon myself
All the hurts and pains of my mothers.

By ensuring that all this remains undefiled
From the stains of the eight mundane concerns,
And by understanding all things as illusions,
I will train myself to be free of the bondage of clinging.

Glossary

ABHIDHARMA (Skt.): one of the three "baskets" of teachings in the Buddhist canon, relating to metaphysics and wisdom.

AFFLICTIVE EMOTIONS (Skt. *klesha*): the minds caused by the fundamental confusion about how things and events exist; the second level of confusion that disturbs our minds and causes suffering.

AGGREGATES, THE FIVE: the traditional Buddhist division of body and mind. The five are form, feeling, discrimination, compositional factors, and consciousness.

ARHAT (Skt.): a practitioner who has achieved the state of no more learning in the individual liberation vehicle.

ARYA (Skt.): a superior being, or one who has gained a direct realization of emptiness.

BODHICHITTA (Skt.): the mind that spontaneously wishes to attain enlightenment in order to benefit others; the fully open and dedicated heart.

BODHISATTVA (Skt.): someone whose spiritual practice is directed toward the achievement of enlightenment for the welfare of all beings; one who possesses the compassionate motivation of bodhichitta.

BODHISATTVAYANA (Skt.): the vehicle of the bodhisattva, or the bodhisattva's path.

BUDDHA, A (Skt.): a fully enlightened being: one who has removed all obscurations veiling the mind and developed all good qualities to perfection; the first of the Three Jewels of refuge.

BUDDHA, THE (Skt.): the historical Buddha, Shakyamuni.

BUDDHA NATURE: the potential the mind has to experience total love and understanding; the most fundamental mind, currently obscured by the afflictive emotions.

BUDDHADHARMA (Skt.): the Buddha's teachings.

CALM ABIDING (Skt. *shamatha*, Tib. *shiné*): meditation for developing single-pointed concentration (Skt. *samadhi*); the mind that is totally free from subtle agitation and subtle dullness.

CESSATION: the end of all suffering, usually references the third of the four noble truths, the truth of the cessation of suffering and its causes.

COLLECTIVE GENERALITY: the way the mind assumes the wholeness of an observed object not actually perceived by direct perception, often causing error.

CONDITIONED EXISTENCE: a synonym for cyclic existence, the way we are trapped in an endless round of rebirths due to the continual ripening of causes and conditions of negative karmic imprints.

CONTRIVED BODHICHITTA: bodhichitta that is induced during meditation but does not have the strength to continue between sessions.

CYCLIC EXISTENCE: *see samsara.*

DEPENDENT ARISING: coming into being in dependence on causes and conditions.

DHARMA (Skt.): literally "that which holds (one back from suffering)"; often refers to the Buddha's teachings, but more generally to anything that helps the practitioner attain liberation; the second of the Three Jewels of refuge.

EMPTINESS (Skt. *shunyata*): the nature of reality: that all phenomena lack (or are "empty" of) intrinsic or inherent existence.

EQUAL-SETTING MIND: the mind free of all dullness or agitation, the ninth and final stage of shamatha meditation.

FOUR NOBLE TRUTHS, THE: the teaching set forth in the first discourse of the Buddha; the four noble truths are: the truth of suffering, the truth of the origin of suffering, the truth of the cessation of suffering, and the truth of the path leading to the cessation of suffering.

GELUG (Tib.): founded by Lama Tsongkhapa, one of the four schools of Tibetan Buddhism; the others are Sakya, Nyingma, and Kagyu.

GESHE (Tib.): the title of a teacher in the Gelug sect who has completed the most extensive monastic and philosophical training.

GOMPA (Tib.): prayer or meditation room in a monastery, literally the place (*pa*) of meditation (*gom*).

GURU PUJA (Skt.): *see Lama Chöpa.*

HEARER: one of the two kinds of arhats (those who have attained the state of no more learning in the individual liberation vehicle), who have achieved arhathood through following a teacher or teachings. The other kind is "pratyekabuddha."

HIGHEST YOGA TANTRA (Skt. *Anuttarayoga Tantra*): the highest among the four classes of tantra; the others are Action (Skt. *Kriya*), Performance (Skt. *Charya*), and Yoga Tantra.

INDIVIDUAL LIBERATION VEHICLE: the vehicle or path that leads to liberation, the ultimate goal of the Theravada tradition.

INDIVIDUAL LIBERATION VOWS (Skt. *pratimoksha*): the vows associated with the individual liberation vehicle; the first of three levels of vows that can be taken, the others being bodhisattva and tantric vows.

INHERENT EXISTENCE: existing from its own side, without depending on causes and conditions.

JEWELS, THE THREE: the common name for the three main refuges in Buddhism, the Buddha, the Dharma, and the Sangha.

KADAM(PA) (Tib.): the earliest of the Tibetan lineages, later integrated into the other four schools, Nyingma, Sakya, Kagyu, and Gelug.

KARMA (Skt.): literally "action," the natural law of cause and effect whereby positive actions produce happiness and negative actions produce suffering.

KARMIC IMPRINT (Tib. *pak chak*): the energy or propensity left by a mental act on the mindstream that will remain until it either ripens into a result or is purified.

LAMA CHÖPA (Tib.) (Skt. *Guru Puja*): the twice-monthly prayer ceremony performed in Gelug organizations to celebrate its founder, Lama Tsongkhapa.

LAMA TSONGKHAPA (1357–1419): a great Tibetan teacher and founder of the Gelug tradition.

LAMRIM (Tib.): the graduated path to enlightenment—the traditional presentation of the Buddha's teachings according to the Gelug school of Tibetan Buddhism.

LAMRIM CHENMO (Tib.): *The Great Treatise on the Stages of the Path to Enlightenment*; the extensive lamrim text written by Lama Tsongkhapa.

MADHYAMAKA (Skt.): the middle way; the highest of the four Indian philosophical schools that are taught in Tibetan monasteries.

MAHAYANA (Skt.): literally "the Great Vehicle," representing one of the two main divisions of Buddhist thought; Mahayana is practiced in Tibet, Mongolia, China, Vietnam, Korea, and Japan; the emphasis of Mahayana thought is on bodhichitta, the wisdom that realizes emptiness, and enlightenment.

MENTAL AFFLICTIONS: *see afflictive emotions*.

NIRVANA (Skt.): a state of freedom from all delusions and karma, having liberated oneself from cyclic existence (samsara).

NOBLE EIGHTFOLD PATH, THE: the various attributes we need to develop to attain freedom from suffering; they are: right speech, right action, right livelihood, right effort, right mindfulness, right concentration, right view, and right thought.

PALI: the ancient Indian language used in the earlier (Theravada) Buddhist canonical texts.

PERVASIVE SUFFERING: the most subtle of the three kinds of suffering, one that pervades our entire existence; the other two are *suffering of suffering* and *suffering of change*.

POISONS, THE THREE: the common name for the three root delusions of ignorance, attachment, and aversion.

PRAJNAPARAMITA (Skt.): the perfection (*paramita*) of wisdom (*prajna*); the body of Mahayana sutras explicitly teaching emptiness, while implicitly teaching the paths of the bodhisattva. The *Heart of Wisdom Sutra* is an example.

PRATIMOKSHA VOWS (Skt.): *see individual liberation vows.*

PRATYEKABUDDHA (Skt.): one of the two kinds of arhats (those who have attained the state of no more learning in the individual liberation vehicle), who have achieved arhathood through their own efforts, without following a teacher or teachings. The other kind is "hearer."

SADHANA (Skt): the meditation manual used in tantric deity yoga practice.

SAMSARA (Skt.): cyclic existence, the state of being constantly reborn due to delusions and karma.

SANSKRIT: the ancient Indian language used in the Mahayana texts.

SCOPES, THE THREE: the three levels of training within the lamrim (gradual path to enlightenment), these being: lower scope, focused on gaining a fortunate rebirth; medium scope, focused on liberation from samsara; and higher scope, focused on full enlightenment.

SEALS, THE FOUR: the basic Buddhist tenets, also called the *four views* or *four axioms.* They are (1) all products are impermanent, (2) all contaminated things are miserable, (3) all phenomena are empty and selfless, and (4) nirvana is peace.

SENTIENT BEING: a being with sentience, any being with a mind that instinctively seeks happiness and the avoidance of suffering.

SHAMATHA (Skt.): *see calm abiding.*

SHASTRA (Skt.): a classical Indian commentary on the teachings of the Buddha.

SUFFERING, THE THREE TYPES OF: one of the ways of classifying suffering in the four noble truths; they are suffering of suffering, suffering of change (the propensity impermanent phenomena have to cause dissatisfaction), and pervasive suffering (the way our whole existence is pervaded with imperfection).

SUTRA (Skt.): an actual discourse of the Buddha.

SUTRAYANA (Skt.): the vehicle of the Mahayana that takes the Buddhist sutras as its main textual source.

TANTRA (Skt.): literally "thread" or "continuity"; a text of esoteric teachings of Buddhism; often refers to the teachings themselves.

TANTRAYANA (Skt.) (also mantrayana, vajrayana): the vehicle of tantra.

TATHAGATA (Skt.): literally "one thus gone"; an epithet for a buddha, especially the historical Buddha.

TENETS: views held to be fundamental to a belief system.

THERAVADA (Skt.): literally, "the way of the elders"; the branch of Buddhism that takes the early Pali canon as its source; also widely known as Hinayana (small vehicle) to contrast it to Mahayana (great vehicle), this term is often considered derogatory.

UNCONTRIVED BODHICHITTA: bodhichitta that occurs spontaneously, both within and outside of meditation sessions.

VAJRAYANA (Skt.): (also mantrayana, tantrayana) the vehicle of tantra.

BIBLIOGRAPHY

Arya Vimuktisena and Haribhadra. *Abhisamayalamkara with Vritti and Aloka*. Trans. by Gareth Sparham. Fremont, CA: Jain Publishing Company, 2006.

Druppa, Gyalwa Gendun. *Training the Mind in the Great Way*. Ithaca, NY: Snow Lion Publications, 1993.

Foundation for the Preservation of the Mahayana Tradition. *Lama Chöpa, Extended Edition*. Taos, NM: FPMT Inc., 2004.

Gyatso, Lobsang. *Bodhicitta: Cultivating the Compassionate Mind of Enlightenment*. Ithaca, NY: Snow Lion Publications, 1997.

Gyatso, Tenzin, the Fourteenth Dalai Lama. *Transforming the Mind: Teachings on Generating Compassion*. London: Thorsons, 2000.

Jinpa, Thupten, trans. *Mind Training: The Great Collection*. Boston: Wisdom Publications, 2005.

Khunu Rinpoche. *Vast as the Heavens, Deep as the Sea: Verses in Praise of Bodhicitta*. Trans. by Gareth Sparham. Boston: Wisdom Publications, 1999.

Garfield, Jay. *The Fundamental Wisdom of the Middle Way: Nagarjuna's Mulamadhyamakakarika*. New York: Oxford University Press, 1995.

Nanamoli, Bhikkhu, and Bhikkhu Bodhi, trans. *Middle Length Discourses of the Buddha: A Translation of the Majjhima Nikaya*. Boston: Wisdom Publications, 1995.

Pabonka Rinpoche. *Liberation in the Palm of Your Hand: A Concise Discourse on the Path to Enlightenment*. Trans. by Michael Richards. Boston: Wisdom Publications, 1991.

Shantideva. *A Guide to the Bodhisattva's Way of Life* (Skt: *Bodhisattvacharyavatara*). Trans. by Stephen Batchelor. Dharamsala, India: Library of Tibetan Works and Archives, 1979.

Tsering, Tashi. *Buddhist Psychology*. Boston: Wisdom Publications, 2006.

———. *The Four Noble Truths*. Boston: Wisdom Publications, 2005.

Tsong kha pa Blo bzang grags pa. *Byang chub lam rim che ba*. Xining: Mtsho sngon mi rigs dpe skrun khang, 1985.

Tsongkhapa, Lama. *Great Treatise on the Stages of the Path to Enlightenment* (*Lamrim Chenmo*). Xining: Mtsho sngon mi rigs dpe skrun khang, 1985.

Zopa Rinpoche, Lama Thubten. *Wish-Fulfilling Golden Sun*. Lama Yeshe Wisdom Archive website. http://www.lamayeshe.com/lama zopa/wfgs/wfgs.shtml (accessed 29 May 2007).

NOTES

1 Shantideva, *A Guide to the Bodhisattva's Way of Life*, trans. Stephen Batchelor, III:32 (Dharamsala, India: Library of Tibetan Works and Archives, 1981), p. 27.

2 Khunu Rinpoche, *Vast as the Heavens, Deep as the Sea*, trans. Gareth Sparham, vv. 70 and 77 (Boston: Wisdom Publications, 1999), p. 49.

3 Ibid., v. 98, p. 59.

4 Shantideva, *A Guide to the Bodhisattva's Way of Life*, I:21–22, p. 7.

5 Ibid., I:7, p. 4.

6 Ibid., I:10, p. 5.

7 *Arhat* is the term used for a practitioner of the individual liberation vehicle who has achieved the final path of the five paths, *no more learning*, or liberation from cyclic existence.

8 Shantideva, *A Guide to the Bodhisattva's Way of Life*, III:36, p. 26.

9 Tsongkhapa, *Lamrim Chenmo*, Mtsho sngon edition (*Byang chub lam rim che ba* [Xining: Mtsho sngon mi rigs dpe skrun khang, 1985]), p. 300. All quotes translated by Geshe Tashi Tsering.

10 Quoted in Gyatso, Lobsang, *Bodhicitta: Cultivating the Compassionate Mind of Enlightenment* (Ithaca, NY: Snow Lion Publications, 1997), p. 18.

11 Shantideva, *A Guide to the Bodhisattva's Way of Life*, VI:2–3, p. 57.

12 Khunu Rinpoche, *Vast as the Heavens*, v. 37, p. 37.

13 Our consciousness is the combination of many mental events happening simultaneously. In Buddhist psychology these are divided into main mind

and mental factors. The main minds are the five sensory main minds (visual, auditory, and so on) and the mental main mind, which can be perceptual or conceptual. The mental factors are all the minds that attend these main minds. For a full explanation, see Tsering, Geshe Tashi, *Buddhist Psychology* (Boston: Wisdom Publications, 2006), pp. 21–42.

14 Quoted in Tsongkhapa, *Lamrim Chenmo*, p. 291.

15 Khunu Rinpoche, *Vast as the Heavens*, v. 140, p. 73.

16 Quoted in Gyatso, *Bodhicitta*, p. 11.

17 For an explanation of mind and mental factors, see Tsering, *Buddhist Psychology*, pp. 21–42.

18 The twelve links of dependent origination is a set of twelve causes and effects that shows the cyclic nature of our life. The twelve links are ignorance, karma, consciousness, name and form, sense bases, contact, feeling, clinging, craving, existence, birth, and aging and death. See Tsering, Geshe Tashi, *The Four Noble Truths* (Boston: Wisdom Publications, 2005), p. 93.

19 Quoted in Zopa Rinpoche, Lama Thubten, *Wish-Fulfilling Golden Sun*, Bodhichitta section. Unpublished manuscript available on Lama Yeshe Wisdom Archive website, http://www.lamayeshe.com/lamazopa/wfgs/wfgs.shtml (accessed 29 May 2007), p. 112.

20 Shantideva, *A Guide to the Bodhisattva's Way of Life*, VI:118, p. 77.

21 Gyatso, Tenzin, the Fourteenth Dalai Lama, *Transforming the Mind: Teachings on Generating Compassion* (London: Thorsons, 2000), p. 73.

22 Tsongkhapa, *Lamrim Chenmo*, p. 303.

23 Ibid., p. 297.

24 Ibid., p. 307.

25 Ibid., p. 307.

26 Khunu Rinpoche, *Vast as the Heavens*, v. 77, p. 51.

27 Shantideva, *A Guide to the Bodhisattva's Way of Life*, I:19, p. 6.

28 Tsongkhapa, *Lamrim Chenmo*, p. 285.

29 Khunu Rinpoche, *Vast as the Heavens*, vv. 338–39, p. 139.

30 Shantideva, *A Guide to the Bodhisattva's Way of Life*, VIII:90–91, p. 113.

31 Gyatso, *Transforming the Mind*, p. 72.

32 Shantideva, *A Guide to the Bodhisattva's Way of Life*, VIII:95–96, p. 114.

33 Ibid., VIII:94, p. 113.

34 Ibid., VIII:155, p. 124.

35 Gyatso, *Transforming the Mind*, p. 75.

36 Shantideva, *A Guide to the Bodhisattva's Way of Life*, VIII:131, p. 120.

37 Ibid., VIII:129–30, p. 119.

38 *Lama Chöpa, Extended Edition*, v. 91 (Taos, NM: FPMT Inc., 2004), p. 83.

39 Shantideva, *A Guide to the Bodhisattva's Way of Life*, VIII:158–59, p. 124.

40 Ibid., VIII:114, p. 117.

41 Tsongkhapa, *Lamrim Chenmo*, p. 313.

42 Jay Garfield, trans., *The Fundamental Wisdom of the Middle Way: Nagarjuna's Mulamadhyamakakarika* (New York: Oxford University Press, 1995).

43 *Nagarjuna's "Commentary on the Awakening Mind"*, September 2007, His Holiness the Dalai Lama: DVD from His Holiness the Dalai Lama's Office, Namgyel Monastery, Dharamsala, India, 2007.

44 *Lama Chöpa*, vv. 95 and 99, pp. 89–91.

45 Pabongka Rinpoche, *Liberation in the Palm of Your Hand: A Concise Discourse on the Path to Enlightenment*, trans. Michael Richards (Boston: Wisdom Publications, 1991), p. 609.

46 Tsongkhapa, *Lamrim Chenmo*, p. 292.

47 Shantideva, *A Guide to the Bodhisattva's Way of Life*, I:15–16, p. 6.

48 Tsongkhapa, *Lamrim Chenmo*, p. 309.

49 See also Gyatso, *Bodhicitta*, pp. 123–28, and Arya Vimuktisena and Haribhadra, *Abhisamayalamkara with Vritti and Aloka*, trans. Gareth Sparham (Fremont, CA: Jain Publishing Company, 2006), pp. 9–16.

50 *Abhisamayalamkara*, p. 10.

51 The twelve deeds of a buddha, according to Tibetan Buddhism, are: descending from Tushita Heaven, entering into his mother's womb, birth, studying arts and handicrafts, enjoying life in the palace, renunciation,

ascetic practices, going to Bodhgaya, defeating the negative forces, enlightenment, turning the wheel of the Dharma, entering parinirvana.

52 I take refuge until I am enlightened in the Buddha, the Dharma, and the Sangha. By the positive potential I create by practicing generosity and the other far-reaching attitudes, may I attain Buddhahood in order to benefit all sentient beings.
Taken from the FPMT Prayer Book, vol 1.

53 O Buddhas, Bodhisattvas and Gurus please listen
To what I now say from the depths of my heart.
Just as all Buddhas of the past have developed
The thought of Enlightenment, true Bodhichitta,
Then practiced its stages of graded development
Following the trainings of all Buddha's Sons,
So may I too, for the sake of all beings,
Develop Bodhichitta and follow the trainings
Exactly as all Bodhisattvas have done.

At this moment my life has become truly fruitful,
For having attained an endowed human body
Today I have developed the true Buddha essence,
Bodhichitta, and thus have become Buddha's Son.

Applying now any skilled means whatsoever
May I always accord what I do with this essence
(And follow the actions of all Buddha's Sons).
May I never confuse with this pure faultless essence
(Any teachings that lack this Enlightening Thought).

Taken from the FPMT Six-Session Guru Yoga, originally from An Extensive Six-Session Yoga by the First Panchen Lama, expanded by Pabongka Rinpoche, trans. Berzin, 1973.

54 Tsongkhapa, Lamrim Chenmo, p. 331.

55 Thupten Jinpa, trans., Mind Training: The Great Collection (Boston: Wisdom Publications, 2005), p. 276.

56 Lama Chöpa, v. 97, p. 89.

57 Shantideva, A Guide to the Bodhisattva's Way of Life, X:55, p. 188.

58 From the FPMT Prayer Book, vol 1.

59 Khunu Rinpoche, Vast as the Heavens, v. 21, p. 31.

60 Quoted in Tsongkhapa's *Lamrim Chenmo*, p. 340.

61 See Lama Zopa's extensive meditation on this in his unpublished book, *Wish-Fulfilling Golden Sun*, which can be found on the Lama Yeshe Wisdom Archive website (http://www.lamayeshe.com/lamazopa/wfgs/wf gs.shtml).

62 Tsongkhapa, *Lamrim Chenmo*, p. 344.

63 Ibid.

64 Ibid., p. 365.

65 Ibid., p. 390.

66 The eight Mahayana precepts are kept for twenty-four hours and are: not killing, not stealing, not lying, not indulging in sexual activity, not eating at inappropriate times, not wearing jewelry or singing or dancing (or activities that increase attachment), not sitting on high or ornate beds (or activities that increase pride), and not taking intoxicants.

67 Shantideva, *A Guide to the Bodhisattva's Way of Life*, V:12–14, p. 39.

68 *Lama Chöpa*, v. 105, p. 93.

69 Khunu Rinpoche, *Vast as the Heavens*, vv. 199 and 203, pp. 91 and 93.

70 *Abhayarajakumara Sutta*, Sutta 58, *Middle Length Discourses of the Buddha: A Translation of the Majjhima Nikaya*, trans. Bhikkhu Nanamoli and Bhikkhu Bodhi (Boston: Wisdom Publications, 1995).

71 Jinpa, *Mind Training*, p. 276.

Index

About the Authors

Geshe Tashi Tsering escaped Tibet in 1959 with his family at the age of one, and entered Sera Mey Monastic University in South India at thirteen, graduating sixteen years later as a Lharampa Geshe, the highest level. Requested by Lama Thubten Zopa Rinpoche, the Spiritual Director of the Foundation for the Preservation of the Mahayana Tradition (FPMT), to teach in the West, he became the resident teacher at Jamyang Buddhist Centre in London in 1994, where he developed the *Foundation of Buddhist Thought*, which has become one of the core courses in the FPMT's education program. He has taught the course in England and Europe since 1997.

Gordon McDougall was director of Cham Tse Ling, the FPMT's Hong Kong center, for two years in the 1980s and worked for Jamyang Buddhist Centre in London from 2000–2006. He helped develop the *Foundation of Buddhist Thought* and now administers it.

FOUNDATION OF BUDDHIST THOUGHT

The Foundation of Buddhist Thought is a two-year course in Buddhist studies created by Geshe Tashi Tsering of Jamyang Buddhist Centre in London. The program draws upon the depth of Tibetan Buddhist philosophy to exemplify how Buddhism can make a real difference in the way we live our lives. *The Foundation of Buddhist Thought* is part of the Foundation for the Preservation of the Mahayana Tradition (FPMT) core study program. This course can be taken either in person or by correspondence. It consists of the following six four-month modules:

+ The Four Noble Truths
+ Relative Truth, Ultimate Truth
+ Buddhist Psychology
+ The Awakening Mind
+ Emptiness
+ Tantra

In addition to the related Wisdom book, each module includes approximately fifteen hours of professionally edited audio teachings on either CD, MP3, or audiotape, taken from Geshe Tashi's most recent London course. These are used in conjunction with guided meditations to explore each topic in depth. Each student is also part of a study group led by a tutor who facilitates discussions twice a month, helping the student to bring the topics to life through active dialogue with other members of the group. Essays and exams are also an essential part of the curriculum. This mixture of reading, listening, meditating, discussing, and writing ensures that each student will gain an understanding and mastery of these profound and important concepts.

A vital aspect of the course is Geshe Tashi's emphasis on the way these topics affect our everyday lives. Even a philosophical topic such as relative and ultimate truth is studied from the perspective of the choices we make on a daily basis, and the way to begin to develop a more realistic approach to living according to the principles of Buddhist thought.

"A real life-changer. The jigsaw that was Dharma all suddenly fits into place." —*course graduate*

To find out more about *The Foundation of Buddhist Thought*, please visit our website at **www.buddhistthought.org**. To find out more about FPMT study programs, please visit **www.fpmt.org**.

About Wisdom

WISDOM PUBLICATIONS, a nonprofit publisher, is dedicated to making available authentic Buddhist works for the benefit of all. We publish translations of the sutras and tantras, commentaries and teachings of past and contemporary Buddhist masters, and original works by the world's leading Buddhist scholars. We publish our titles with the appreciation of Buddhism as a living philosophy and with the special commitment to preserve and transmit important works from all the major Buddhist traditions.

To learn more about Wisdom, or to browse books online, visit our website at wisdompubs.org. You may request a copy of our mail-order catalog online or by writing to:

> Wisdom Publications
> 199 Elm Street
> Somerville, Massachusetts 02144 USA
> Telephone: (617) 776-7416 ✦ Fax: (617) 776-7841
> Email: info@wisdompubs.org
> www.wisdompubs.org

The Wisdom Trust

As a nonprofit publisher, Wisdom is dedicated to the publication of fine Dharma books for the benefit of all sentient beings and dependent upon the kindness and generosity of sponsors in order to do so. If you would like to make a donation to Wisdom, please do so through our Somerville office. If you would like to sponsor the publication of a book, please write or email us at the address above.

Thank you.

Wisdom is a nonprofit, charitable 501(c)(3) organization affiliated with the Foundation for the Preservation of the Mahayana Tradition (FPMT).

Also available from the
Foundation of Buddhist Thought Series

The Four Noble Truths
Foundation of Buddhist Thought, Volume 1
Geshe Tashi Tsering
192 pages | ISBN 0861712706 | $14.95

In this, the first volume of the *Foundation of Buddhist Thought*, Geshe Tashi provides a complete presentation the Buddha's seminal Four Noble Truths, which summarize the fundamentals of the Buddhist worldview. Indeed, they are an essential framework for understanding all of the other teachings of the Buddha.

Buddhist Psychology
Foundation of Buddhist Thought, Volume 3
Geshe Tashi Tsering
176 pages | ISBN 0861712722 | $14.95

Buddhist Psychology addresses both the nature of the mind and how we know what we know. Just as scientists observe and catalog the material world, Buddhists for centuries have been observing and cataloging the components of our inner experience. The result is a rich and subtle knowledge that can be harnessed to the goal of increasing human well-being.